Copyright Notice	*.2*
Getting Ready	*..3*
Potted History	*..5*
The Maps	*..8*
The Walks	*...8*
Walk 1 - St Nicholas and the Cathedral	*...........................9*
Walk 2 – The Markets and the Castle	*..........................55*
Walk 3 - Along the Canals	*.. 100*
Did you enjoy these walks?	*.. 126*
Other Strolling Around Books to try:	*......................... 127*

Copyright Notice

Strolling Around Ghent by Irene Reid

ISBN: 9798622481710

All rights reserved. This book may not be reproduced in any form, in whole or in part, without written permission from the author.

The author has made every effort to ensure the accuracy of the information in this book at the time of going to press, and cannot accept responsibility for any consequences arising from the use of the book.

Book Cover
Photo by Irene Reid

Enhanced by Prisma Photo Editor

Getting Ready

If you reach Ghent out of the main season, you will unfortunately find some of the "sights" closed. Of course the main attractions will be open all year, but it is frustrating to reach a museum or a church to find the door locked. So it's worth checking the schedules before you book your trip.

Avoid exploring Ghent on a Monday as most sights will be closed. Another thing worth taking note of is that most sights will not open before 10:00am earliest. So if you are an early riser have a leisurely breakfast. Also some of the less visited sights will open in the afternoon only. You can get all the opening hours at one of the tourist offices.

The Ghent City Card

You should also decide whether to purchase a City Card. Whether it's worthwhile depends on what you actually want to visit. If you were to visit all the sights on these walks, then it is definitely a worthwhile investment.

You can buy the card at the tourist office in the Old Fish Market. You can see details about what is included here.

http://www.visitgent.be/en/citycard-gent

You can buy a 2 day card or a 3 day card. The card clock starts ticking when you first use it to visit any of the included sights. So if you use it at 14:00 on day 1 of your holiday, it will expire at 14:00 on day 2 or 3 of your holiday.

The City Card also gives you use of unlimited public transport for the same number of days. It's a little confusing however, because using the card on public transport has no connection to using it to see the sights. Simply write the date that you first use it on public transport on the back of the card. You can then use it for transport for 1 or 2 more days after that. The time of day of use is irrelevant.

Potted History

Archeologists have dug up evidence of people living in the Ghent area from prehistoric times. It lies where the rivers Lys and Scheldt meet, and many historians think Ghent is a derivation of "ganda", an old Celtic word which means confluence.

Ghent didn't really appear in any written document until the seventh century, when St Bavo's Abbey was founded by the French missionary Saint Amand, who arrived to convert the natives to Christianity. However the locals preferred their own pagan gods, so they usually beat up or slaughtered any preacher foolish enough to venture near them. Surprisingly Amand survived and although he was beaten up a few times, he did convert them to Christianity and his abbey thrived.

Ghent was then a victim to Viking raids like most settlements along northern Europe, but it survived and grew into a thriving town. The merchants bought in wool from Scotland and England, wove it into luxurious cloths, and shipped them across Europe at a healthy profit.

Ghent at this time was more or less a self-ruling independent city state, but it was also part of Flanders which was ruled by the Duke of Burgundy. It was in fact only second in size to Paris.

The hundred year's war erupted and was a long drawn out affair between England and France over the succession to the French throne in the fourteenth century. England had been conquered by the French after the battle of Hastings way back in 1066, and the English Royal family was still directly related to the French Royal family. So when the French Royal family didn't have a direct heir to the throne, both the French relatives and the English relatives made a claim, and ended up with both countries going to war.

Eventually after sitting on the fence for as long as possible Ghent favoured England, which was a pity because France eventually won. France started to tax wealthy Ghent as much as they could. The Ghent Guilds revolted and the City rose up in arms; Ghent lost that battle, many men, and some pride, but at least the city survived.

Years rolled by and Flanders was inherited by one branch of the ruling French family after another, until finally it was inherited by the Hapsburgs who were Austrian and also ruled Spain.

The Hapsburg family's most famous son was Charles V, the Holy Roman Emperor. He was actually born in Ghent in 1500. When he donned the crown he promptly started taxing Ghent to the hilt, and once again the Guilds were up in arms. Charles responded by ordering his huge Spanish army to march through France and up to the gates of Ghent. Ghent wisely surrendered, and Charles decided to humiliate his city rather than punish it.

The city lords and leaders were assembled, their shoes were removed, a noose was hung round their necks, and they were marched up to the castle to meet their fate. Charles let them live, but as punishment he removed all Ghent's privileges which the city had worked so hard to achieve. Ghent went into a spiral of decline. To commemorate that day, the locals re-enact the march of the Stroppendragers (noose carriers) every summer.

Ghent managed to recover its market in the eighteenth century when Lieven Bauwens pinched the design for the Spinning Mule, a weaving machine, from England. Seeing a golden opportunity, Ghent produced the machines rapidly and shot into the Industrial Revolution, again making cloth for all of Europe.

In the nineteenth century the huge Ghent-Terneuzen canal was constructed to the north of the city, to give Ghent better access to the Scheldt estuary. At that time Flanders was part of the Netherlands. However Ghent's bishop raised the question of why Ghent and other Flemish towns should be part of the Netherlands, and Ghent played a significant role in the 1830 Belgian revolution.

Eventually Belgium was formed but Ghent had made an enemy of the Netherlands. The Dutch responded by blockading the vital canal and the river Scheldt, and once again the cloth industry collapsed. Ghent went into hibernation before re-emerging only last century when the Scheldt and the canal were opened once again. The canal was later enlarged to let today's huge container ships reach the port.

The Maps

There are maps sprinkled all through the walks to help you find your way. If you need to check where you are at any point during a walk, always flip back to find the map you need.

To help you follow the maps, each map shows its start point. In addition numbered directions have been placed on each map. The numbers correspond to the directions within the walks.

The Walks

There are three walks around old Ghent. If you are limited in time, try to fit in Walk 1 and Walk 3.

The three walks actually form a circuit, so you could start with any one of them and just follow the instructions to continue onto the next one.

Walk 1 – St Nicholas and the Cathedral (1.8km)

This walk takes you to the Saint Nicholas church, the Cathedral, the Bell Tower and ends at the Town Hall. Those will probably be the busiest sights you will visit in Ghent.

Walk 2 - The Markets and the Castle (2.1km)

This walk takes you north to see some of the lesser known sights. You then visit the castle and the fish market.

Walk 3 – Along the Canals (1.2km)

This walk takes you along the waterways which are the prettiest part of Ghent, and then returns you to the Saint Nicholas Church.

Walk 1 - St Nicholas and the Cathedral

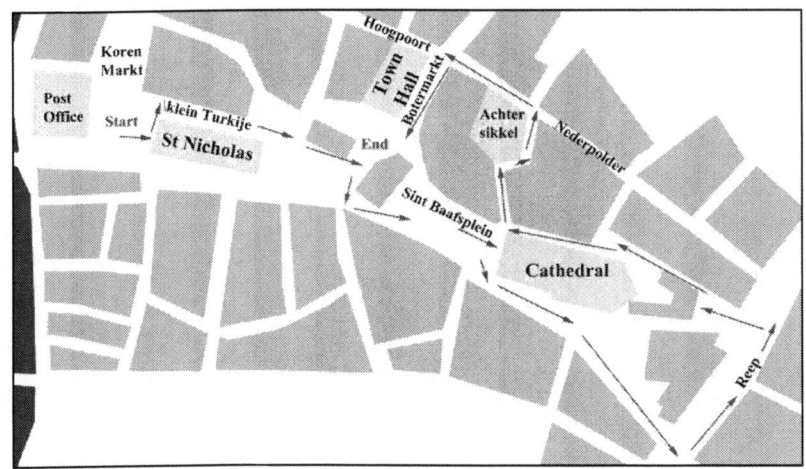

Walk Overview

This walk starts in The KorenMarkt, a large square in the centre of old Ghent which has roads leading off in various directions.

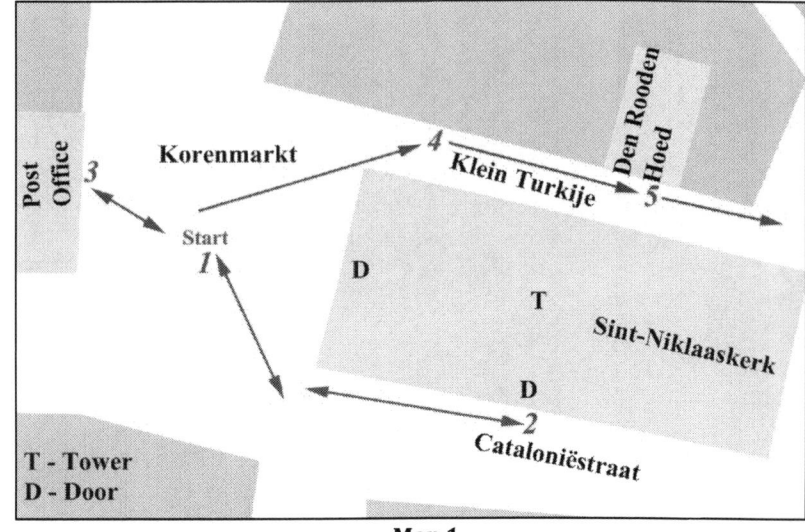
Map 1

KorenMarkt

The square's name tells you this used to be the grain market, where cargoes arriving via the river Scheldt were sold in the Middle Ages.

Saint Nicholas church

The easiest building to identify is the huge Saint Nicholas church, which stands at one end of the square and is built from a grey-blue stone from Tournai. Tournai lies in south Belgium but also on the river Scheldt, so the heavy stone could be transported by boat right into the centre of Ghent.

When Ghent became an important trading centre, the town imposed a tax on all grain merchants who passed through the city – a hefty 25% of their goods. The profits Ghent made from that tax paid for this church, and since Saint Nicholas is the patron saint of sailors, bakers, and traders, it was decided to name the church after him.

This trading connection also prompted Ghent's trade guilds to have their own little chapels added to the church in the fourteenth century. It showed off their importance to the town and a direct line to God was always handy. There was also an element of competition between the guilds and wealthy patrons who all donated beautiful furnishings and carvings

However, Catholic churches suffered badly at the hands of the Protestants during the iconoclasm – a chaotic period of the sixteenth century when the Flemish Protestants decided to destroy images and works of art in the Catholic churches. Many of the statues and paintings in this church were destroyed, including those in the trade guild chapels. The church was attacked again during the French revolution and at one point suffered the indignity of being turned into a horse stable. Later many small houses were constructed using the church wall as a handy pre-fabricated back wall.

The result was that the church deteriorated badly over the centuries. Huge cracks appeared in the walls, so the windows were bricked up to try to stabilize them. Finally in the nineteenth century, Ghent decided that the church was either coming down or it was going to be saved. Happily it was saved. The buildings surrounding it were removed, and since the twentieth century it has been slowly restored.

If you stand in the square in front of the church and look up you can't actually see the church tower, because unusually the tower rises in the middle of the church. It was also used as the town's watchtower and housed the town bells until a separate belfry was built. The church is very old and is worth a visit. The church is often used as an exhibition centre, so you never know what might be on display inside.

Map 1.1 – Make your way towards the front of the church.

At the time of writing the main door is being used as the entrance to a digital tourist attraction. So go round the right hand side of the church, along Cataloniëstraat, to find the entrance to the church – entrance is free.

The Tower and Pulpit

As you enter you will see the bell-tower rising above you, right in the middle of the church. If you are lucky and it is a sunny day, you will find sunlight filtering down from the tower lighting up the interior.

Beneath the tower stands the beautiful double-stair pulpit. Supporting the pulpit you can see the four evangelists, each depicted on a scroll as their symbol. The lion for St Mark, the eagle for St John, the bull for St Luke, and finally a man for St Matthew.

On the pulpit corners are four cherubs holding symbols of the four elements, flowers for earth, an eagle for air, a fish for water and a torch for fire.

Obiits

Spot the diamond shaped paintings which have a coat of arms and the word "obiit" on them - they run from the floor to the ceiling on the church columns.

"Obiit" means "He Died" and they marked the graves of wealthy parishioners. Many Obiits are still stored away waiting their turn for restoration.

Now stand with the door you entered by behind you, and the pulpit in front of you.

The Organ

On your left is a door which should lead into the part of the church which contains its organ. However as already mentioned, that part of the church is currently off limits. It's a shame because if you know anything about organs you might want a closer look.

It was built by Aristide Cavaillé-Coll who was a very famous French organ-maker. When it was first played in the mid-nineteenth century the locals were astonished at the immense sounds which rumbled from their new organ.

When the church restoration started, the precious organ was protected by a huge wooden box. For fifty years it remained out of sight as the church was slowly saved. Finally in 2010 its wooden shield was dismantled, the organ was cleaned, and once again it could be seen by visitors. Sadly it has stayed silent as it too needs a vast restoration.

Ghent has been trying to raise the funds since then to restore the organ. At the time of writing, good progress has been made but the restoration is not yet complete.

So turn right and step into the nave. As you do, take a look at the painting above you and on your right-hand side. It celebrates Saint Nicholas's most famous miracle.

Saint Nicholas

During a great famine an evil butcher killed three children, cut them up, and put the pieces in a barrel of brine to pickle and sell off as hams.

Saint Nicholas was visiting the town during the pickling process and somehow knew what had been done. He opened the barrel and resurrected the three children. So look up to see the little children popping out of their barrel.

The Disciples

Now walk around the perimeter of the church.

The church has an impressive set of statues of the disciples, each holding his associated biblical symbol. You will find them standing right round the perimeter. Some are easy to identify, e.g. Saint Andrew with his saltire cross, and Saint Peter with his key.

The Altar

At the far end of the nave stands the altar. Behind it are four swirling columns which border another painting of Saint Nicholas.

It tells the story of how Nicholas became the Bishop of Myra. The Bishop of Myra died and the Church sent a posse of bishops to Myra to pick someone to fill the position.

While there, the most senior bishop had a vision. It told him to select the first person named Nicholas who entered the church the next morning. He informed his fellow bishops of his vision, so they all waited expectantly by the door next morning. Of course Nicholas walked through it, and was immediately appointed as the new Bishop of Maya.

He is the figure on the left of the painting. He is backing away as his hand is seized by the senior bishop who proclaims him as the new Bishop of Myra.

Above the altar is a statue, once again showing us Saint Nicholas and the lucky three children he saved.

Map 1.2 - Once back outside, turn right to return to the KorenMarkt.

Stand with the church main door behind you. The grand building directly opposite you is the old post office.

The Old Post Office

It's an interesting fact that all over Europe, the postal service in the nineteenth century was seen as important enough to be sited in grand buildings on central sites. Ghent is no different. In 1913 Ghent hosted a world exhibition, and the Post Office was built that year as part of the celebrations.

The post office has a clock tower which might look familiar – that's because it's a replica of Big Ben in London, and its nickname is Little Ben.

If you look up you can see various faces and statues looking back down at you. These are thought to be the city fathers of the time, and the important heads of state who visited Ghent during the exhibition.

Look up to the top right-hand corner and you will see a female statue standing above the heads of state – some believe that is Florence Nightingale.

Sadly the postal service across the world is far less significant now, so this grand building was sold off to private hands. After a brief life as a shopping centre it lay derelict for many years, but has now been restored and the upper floors have reopened as a luxury hotel - visitors can even book a room up in the bell-tower, which must give wonderful views. There is also a cocktail bar called The Cobbler which might tempt you in the evenings.

If you have time, pop into the ground floor to see how the post office has been transformed.

The ground floor is full of shops occupying the spaces which used to sell stamps or send telegrams. You can wander around and see what remains of the original gleaming iron work and wall decoration. Look up to spot the carrier pigeons painted on the wall above the door – they symbolise the speedy dispatch of messages across the country.

Map 1.3 – Once back outside, walk towards the front of Saint Nicholas again. Go up the left hand side of the church into Klein Turkije.

Klein Turkije

This little street has a lovely line of step-gabled houses on the left-hand side.

Its name has nothing to do with turkeys or Turkey. It is apparently derived from the Flemish expression 'ter keie', which means "to the ground". If you went bankrupt all your goods were sold to pay off your debts, and any large items such as furniture were placed on this street for public sale – a kind of enforced garage sale.

Map 1.4 - Walk along Klein Turkije to reach the elderly grey building on the left hand side – it's the second last building on Klein Turkije.

Den Rooden Hoed

This was a thirteenth century inn called Den Rooden Hoed. At one point Albrecht Durer stayed there and there is a plaque commemorating his stay.

Durer was one of the greatest painters of the fifteenth century, and his paintings are treasured in museums across Europe and the world.

He was in Ghent as court painter to Charles V, the Holy Roman Emperor. Whilst in town he visited Saint Bavo's Cathedral to see the "The Adoration of the Mystic Lamb" which you will see shortly. He is quoted as saying it was "a stupendous painting".

Map 1.5 - Continue along Klein Turkije past the church to reach a square called Goudenleeuwplein.

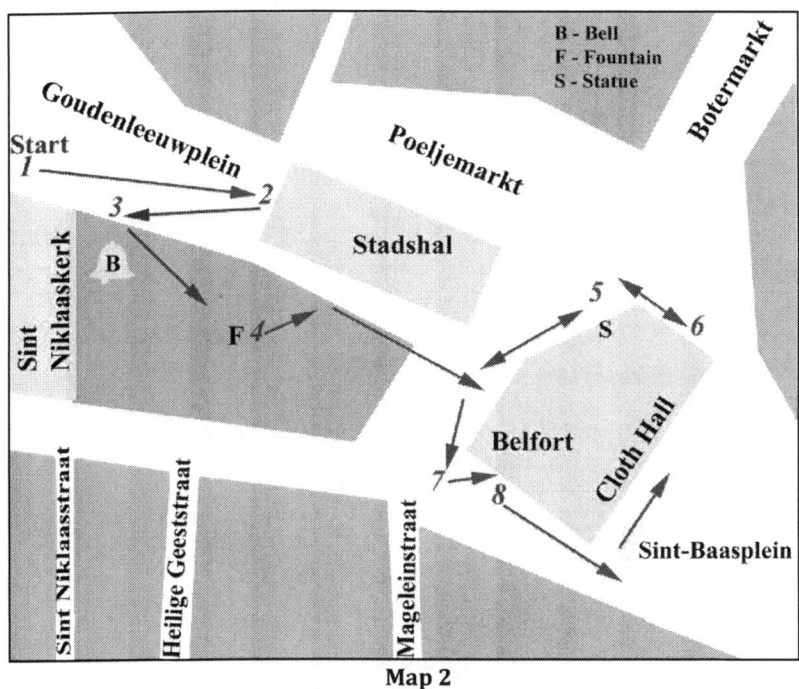
Map 2

The area in front of you, between Saint Nicholas and the Belfry was demolished as part of the Expo preparations in 1913. It was never redeveloped and left Ghent with a large concrete wilderness which was populated by that curse of modern cities, the car.

Recently it was decided to try to repair the damage, and a competition was announced to design a building to fill the square. The modern building in the middle of the square, the Stadshal, was the winner.

Map 2.1 – Walk across Goudenleeuwplein to have a look inside the Stadshal.

Stadshal

Officially the building is called the Stadshal, but it's nicknamed the Schaapstal (sheep-pen). Have a wander under it to see its unique wooden roof. It's made of Aformosia, an endangered hardwood from West Africa; a surprising choice for a forward thinking European city to make!

The sheep-pen has a lot of critics, who complain that it blocks the view of the old buildings and that it is out of place. However it is surely better than a concrete wilderness, but make your own mind up. It's worth visiting at night when it's lit up.

Map 2.2 - Turn to walk back towards Saint Nicholas again. Pause when you reach a plinth with a large bell on it.

De Maagd

The plinth is decorated with a rather small fresco of De Maagd, The Virgin, but it's probably unlike any other image of the Virgin you will have ever seen, as this one has laser beams shooting from her eyes.

The artist, Michaël Borremans, comes from Ghent, and he gave this little work of art to his city. As he worked on the fresco he wiped his brushes on the plinth just to the right of The Virgin, and they were left there as part of the painting.

Unfortunately no-one told the city cleaning department, and they did their very best to remove the brush-strokes. The artist was consulted and decided not to try to reproduce them, so now we have De Maagd minus the brush-strokes.

The Grote Triomphante

The bell on the plinth is called the Grote Triomphante and it used to hang in the belfry - you can read about its demise as you explore the Belfry shortly.

Map 2.3 - Walk down into the sunken green area on your left-hand side using the steps beside the bell.

You will see a fountain in the middle of this little park, often surrounded by students.

The Fountain of Kneeling Youths

This little bronze fountain of five slender boys kneeling and staring into the water has been here for over a century. It's by Georges Minne, a local sculptor who was a colleague of that great sculptor, Rodin. There is a replica in the Parliament Garden in Brussels, but this is the original.

The locals have a nickname for the fountain, "The Peeing boys", which seems an ugly name for a lovely fountain. Rubbing their feet is supposed to bring good luck and eternal youth.

Belfort Dragon

With the bell behind you, look up to the high tower in front of you – that's the belfry.

Ghent started to build the belfry in 1313. You can see a golden dragon weather-vane looking out over the city. It's a copy; the original which is made of 400 kilos of valuable copper is safely inside and you will see it soon.

Map 2.4 - Leave the garden by the stairs on the other side of the park beneath the Belfort (belfry).

Once you are out of the garden, turn left to reach the corner of the building in front of you. You will find a little curved building.

Mammelokker

This little building was a small prison which was bolted onto the side of the larger Cloth hall in 1741. Its odd name translates as "breast sucker".

Look high above the doorway to see the story of Cimon and his daughter Pero. He was imprisoned and condemned to death by starvation, but was saved by his daughter who breastfed him!!

The authorities eventually became puzzled by their prisoner's refusal to die, so the guards were ordered to monitor his visitors and they reported what they saw to the judge. The judge was incredulous and decided to watch himself the next day. When he confirmed what he had been told, he had Pero arrested and brought before him. When asked how she could do it, she fell to her knees and said:

> I did that in the faith of God

The judge was touched and impressed by her faith and fatherly love, so he freed Cimon.

Perhaps Steinbeck had this tale in mind when he wrote the ending of The Grapes of Wrath. Rose of Sharon had just lost her baby and when she finds a starving man she breastfed him to keep him alive.

There is a Mammelokker beer now which you could try in one of Ghent's many bars.

Map 2.5 - Continue walking around the corner in the same direction to reach the entrance of the Cloth Hall.

Cloth Hall

As you already know, cloth and wool were the most important trades in medieval Ghent. This Cloth Hall was added to the side of the belfry and was where the merchandise was stored and traded. By law cloth and wool could only be traded in this building.

The building has a cellar and two storeys. The cellar was where the tools of the trade were stored, the ground floor was for everyday fabrics, and the top floor was for expensive and exclusive fabrics.

Interestingly the Guilds enforced a gender split in the Cloth Hall. Women were only allowed to sell the cheaper fabrics, whereas men could sell anything and also deal with the foreign merchants. Another odd fact is that, the floor space which women were allocated in the hall was for life, and the right to trade would be passed from mother to daughter.

You can pop in to see the beautiful vaulted ceiling.

Map 2.6 – With the Cloth Hall door behind you, turn left to retrace your steps around the building. Make your way past the Mammelokker to reach the corner of the Belfort on Cataloniëstraat.

Map 2.7 - The stairs to the Belfort entrance are a few steps along Cataloniëstraat. If you don't have a City Card, you can buy an entrance ticket in the room below the stairs.

Note, If you don't wish to climb the Belfry Tower, continue this walk from "To Sint Baafsplein" on page 27.

Belfort

Secure Room

You will be directed to go downstairs into the Secure Room.

One of the tower's most important roles was the safety of the city's Privileges. These were the charters which specified the rights the City had earned from Flanders, e.g. the right to hold a market. In those days such documents were priceless and so had to be safely guarded.

Ghent's privileges were stashed in an iron chest which was chained to the ground in the vaulted Secure Room. They entered that room in 1402 and stayed there until 1539. That was when Lille took over as the chief city in this part of Flanders, and as a result all the state documents were transferred there. In 1578 Ghent got its documents back, but the city fathers decided to place them in the Town Hall so they never returned to the Secure Room.

In the room you can see down into a lower chamber which the Germans added during WWII. There was a series of tunnels which they used as shelter from bombs. At the moment the secure room is being guarded by four Watchmen of The Tower. They used to stand high over the city but are now here for safety and have been replaced with copies.

The Dragon

Follow the signs to enter the elevator room, but before you go up have a look at the dragon – it's not very impressive really when you see it up close, but when it was at the top of the tower it would have seemed enormous. It was the guardian of those precious charters and documents.

The Bells

Take the lift to the top.

If access is open, don't miss going up the final little flight of steps to peep into the bell chamber itself. There are 54 bells but you can only see one or two from the doorway. The biggest of them all was Roland which was put in the Belfry in 1325. If a fire was spotted by the eagle-eyed Watch, they would peel out an alarm using Roland. Roland sadly was destroyed by the French King Charles V, to punish Ghent for their rebellion over taxes.

Grote Triomphante

Roland's remains were later used to cast 37 bells of the current 54 bell carillon. One of those was Triomphante, the new major bell which you saw down in the park. Triomphante was last rung in 1914 but tragically cracked and so had to be removed. There are still plans to fix it and return it to the belfry. Robert was the last bell to join the carillon in 1993. The bells peel out every fifteen minutes, so you might see them in action. Return to the elevator floor

The Watch

Step outside to enjoy the view over the city and imagine The Watch doing the same.

The Belfry took over the task of watch-tower from the tower of Saint Nicholas. Most people think the Watch watched for invading armies, but in fact their most important job was to watch for fire, as a fire could wipe out a town built of wood in very little time.

The Carillon

The next floor down contains the carillon itself. Every day the clock is wound up by hoisting the weight of the carillon up, and gravity then takes over. Just like a music box the turning drum pulls the cords to ring the bells. It's worth hanging around for fifteen minutes to see it in action. They reset the pins every two years to new tunes just before Easter Sunday.

The final floor contains a host of little bells which can make a nice photograph. You can ping them to pick out a tune.

Finally you will reach the Secure Room again, so find the steps to return to the entrance hall and exit.

To Sint Baafsplein

Map 2.8 – With the belfry door behind you, turn left to walk around the building and reach the front of the Cloth Hall. It sits on a square called Sint-Baafsplein.

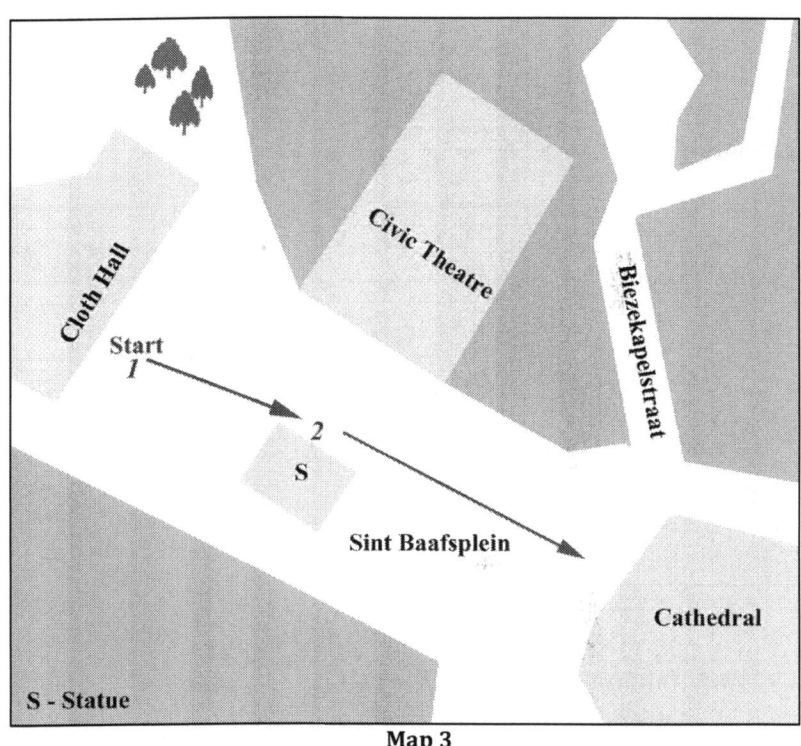

Map 3

Map 3.1 - Cross the square to reach the fountain.

Jan Frans Willems

The fountain and statue in this square is a memorial to Jan Frans Willems, a Flemish writer who fought vociferously for the Flemish language to have complete equality with French.

He was part of the first Flemish Spelling Commission whose task was to standardize the Flemish language, as it was spelled in a myriad of ways. He also published popular items in Flemish to encourage reading and writing – including the mediaeval tale of Reynard the Fox. He organised libraries, concerts, and plays, all to build the Flemish language.

The statue shows a young man who represents the Flemish Movement, liberating the Flemish virgin by removing her blindfold.

On the base is a medallion of Willems and on the sides we see the Flemish anthem and a fox representing his most popular translation, Reynard the Fox.

Ghent's population turned out in their thousands as this statue was unveiled - a procession of people over a kilometre long walked past. So many languages have been lost or are dying out, so it's nice to see one which has survived.

Stand face to face with the figures on the statue. Behind you is Ghent's civic theatre.

Civic Theatre

Fittingly, most of the productions at this theatre are in Flemish. It was commissioned at the end of the nineteenth century as a Flemish theatre, in contrast to the Ghent Opera house where productions were always in French. The new theatre opened in 1899.

Right at the top is a statue of Harmonia, the goddess of Harmony. Beneath her on the pediment is a colourful mosaic of Apollo who is the God of music, accompanied by his muses.

Map 3.2 – Facing the theatre, turn right to cross the square. On the other side of the square stands Saint Bavo's Cathedral which you should make your way to.

St Bavo's Cathedral

This is one of the highlights of your walk through Ghent.

So who was Saint Bavo, you might be asking yourself? He was born near Liege into a noble family, and he was a typical young man of his class, cruel and selfish. Apparently he liked to sell his servants as slaves to other noble families. He married but his beloved wife died and that was the point at which he reformed. He became a monk and gave all his wealth to the poor.

On one of his pilgrimages he came upon one of the servants he had sold into slavery and he was overcome with remorse. He had the man lead him in chains to jail. He died in the original Abbey of St Bavo and he became the patron saint of Ghent. The abbey ruins still exist but are some distance away and not included on these walks. You could visit them later if you have time and interest.

Go inside the Cathedral by whichever door is currently in use by tourists. You can see part of the cathedral for free, and it's worth looking around as it is very beautiful.

Walk down the central nave first to find the pulpit on your right.

The Pulpit of Truth

It's made of black and white marble entwined with oak and is really eye-catching. It's called the Pulpit of Truth and was made by Laurent Delvaux who came from Ghent.

The Tree of Knowledge shelters the pulpit and beneath it are two statues. The elder on the left is Time and he is gazing at the woman on the right. She is Truth and she is reading from a book which says

> "Get up, you who sleep,
> and arise from the dead,
> and Christ will illuminate you"

There are two angels at the foot of the twin stairs; one is gazing up to the pulpit while the other points to it. The place where Truth is told – the pulpit of course!

Explore the rest of the Cathedral. Eventually you will reach a roped off area which can only be accessed by purchasing one of the tickets to see the Ghent Altarpiece. If you don't wish to see it, jump to "Leaving the Cathedral" on page 39 to continue.

A choice

There are two options on how to visit the Ghent Altarpiece. You can simply buy a standard ticket which will let you see the altarpiece and explore the roped off area of the cathedral. This is the cheapest option.

Alternatively you can buy a ticket to visit the crypt and view the "augmented reality" tour first. The tour is in various languages and there is a choice of three levels of detail. Eventually you leave the technology behind and get to see the actual altarpiece.

Make sure you pick up the little leaflet which will describe the sections of the altarpiece when you eventually reach it.

Once through the ticket check you will re-enter the church, and as you do you will find the cathedral's second most famous painting:

The Conversion of St Bavo – Rubens

This is "The Conversion of St Bavo" by Rubens which has had a chequered past.

It was originally commissioned by the bishop of the Cathedral, and Rubens eagerly set to work on its design. Unfortunately that bishop died and the next two bishops ignored Rubens's letters, preferring to place a statue on the altar rather than a painting – perhaps the cost was too much.

The fourth bishop took a different view as he was a fan of Rubens. Rubens was finally able to complete his painting and have it installed as the altarpiece. Rubens was so grateful to that bishop that he added his coat of arms to the painting, and you can see it bottom left.

This all happened in the seventeenth century but the painting has had several homes over the centuries. At the end of the eighteenth century it was "acquired" by the French and taken to Paris. In the early nineteenth century it moved to Brussels – at least the right country! Five years later it returned to Ghent but was stuck in a museum. Finally in 1825 it returned home. It has been recently restored.

It shows us two key events in the life of Saint Bavo. The lower section shows him giving his wealth to the poor after his conversion, and the upper section shows him entering the monastery.

Spot the wonderfully over-the-top headwear of one of the ladies on the left – it was very popular style in Flanders at the time the painting was produced.

It's believed that Rubens used the face of his first wife Isabella Brant for this figure - she died of the plague at just 34. Her companion in the red dress is thought to be Rubens' second wife Helena Fourment – who was very much younger than Rubens when they married. She was just 16 and he was 53 – but that was not seen as unusual in those days.

Augmented Reality

Moving on you will reach the entrance to the crypt. If you have purchased the Augmented Reality ticket, you should enter here.

Finally, with or without the Augmented Reality ticket, you will reach the star of the show.

The Ghent Altarpiece - Jan and Hubert van Eyck

Apart from its artistic merit, it has an intriguing history of survival.

The Iconoclasm
During the Iconoclasm, the Protestants attacked catholic churches and destroyed many paintings and statues.

The Ghent altarpiece would have suffered the same fate; however the church took it apart and hid the paintings in a room in the Cathedral tower. The iconoclasts burst into the cathedral using a battering ram, but didn't find the precious paintings.

When the coast was clear the church had them removed to the Town Hall where they lay safe until the destruction had stopped.

Napoleon
Napoleon was very fond of stripping the cities he conquered of their fine art and shipping it to Paris. The Ghent Altarpiece was of course included and ended up in the Musée Napoléon, and they stayed there until 1816 when Napoleon was defeated and his loot was returned to the liberated countries.

Astonishingly Ghent became indifferent to the Ghent Altarpiece and sold part of it to a London art dealer, and he then sold several of the panels to Berlin.

World War I
During WWI the Germans took the chance to pinch the Ghent panels to complete the set. However, the Versailles Treaty at the end of that war stated that not only the panels which had been nicked should be returned, but as recompense Germany had to give up their own panels to Belgium as well. The Germans had no choice, but it rankled badly.

Between the wars
One of the panels, The Just Judges, was stolen from the Cathedral between the wars in 1934. All that was left was a note which said:

> Taken from Germany by the Treaty of Versailles.

The thief then started a negotiation with the Belgian Government, demanding a million francs for its return. The deal was never completed.

Then a man called Arsène Goedertier suffered a stroke, and on his deathbed claimed that he was the thief and would never reveal where the panel was hidden. His last clue was a note:

> It rests in a place where neither I, nor anybody else, can take it away without arousing the attention of the public.

The panel has never been found and what you see now is a copy. Perhaps someday it will turn up.

World War II
When WW II started, Belgium tried to send the panels to the Vatican for safety. However they were en route through Italy when Italy decided to join the war. Hitler demanded that the paintings were brought to Bavaria and they were stashed in a castle. When the allies started bombing Germany, the paintings were moved again into a salt mine for safety. They were finally rescued by the US army and returned to Ghent.

So it's astonishing that the Ghent Altarpiece now stands before us with only "The Just Judges" missing.

Once you leave the altarpiece you can explore the rest of the roped-off section of the cathedral.

There is one more painting to find. It's in the chapel of St Nickolas which is very near the end of the roped-off section.

Christ among the Scribes – Frans Pourbus

It shows a famous event from the bible. A very young Jesus sits in the middle of a crowd of learned men, who are amazed at his knowledge.

What is interesting is that the artist included some very important personages of the day in the crowd – Emperor Charles V stands hand on hip at the front on the left side. His son, King Philip II of Spain, is seated on his right.

When you have had enough, leave the cathedral and return to Sint-Baafsplein.

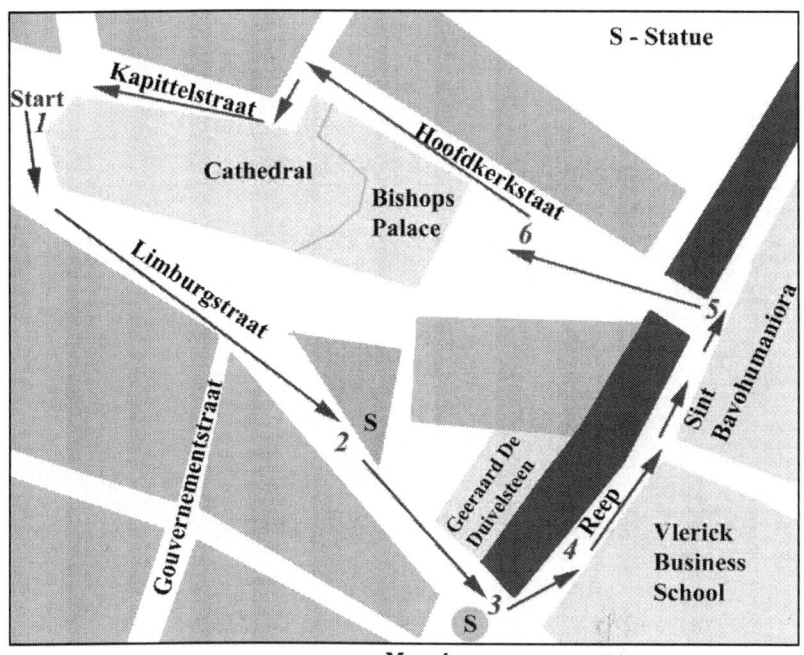

Map 4

Leaving the Cathedral

Map 4.1 – With the cathedral behind you, turn left to walk around it and then along Limburgstraat. You will pass Gouvernementstraat on your right.

Follow the tram lines down the street and you will reach a grassy area on your left which holds a large memorial statue.

Van Eyck brothers monument

This monument to the Van Eyck brothers was created for the 1913 World Expo. Fittingly, it was placed near the Cathedral as it holds the brothers' greatest work. Hubert is on the left and is holding a bible with his brushes at his feet, while Jan holds his paint palette on the right.

There are often flowers left at this memorial by fans.

Map 4.2 - Continue along Limburgstraat toward Ghent's second castle, Geeraard De Duivelsteen. Walk past what's left of the castle moat to reach a crossroads.

Lieven Bauwens

The statue you see on your right is Lieven Bauwens. He is the chap who stole the design plans of the revolutionary Spinning Mule when he visited England.

The Spinning Mule was an improvement on the Spinning Jenny, the spinning machine which was invented in England and which let spinners produce far more thread than previously.

Bauwens smuggled the plans back to Ghent and reignited Ghent's own textiles industry.

Map 4.3 - Turn left along the front of the castle and its moat to see the castle to its best advantage.

Geeraard De Duivelsteen (Geeraard the Devil Castle)

The castle is named after its founder, Sir Geeraard, who was nicknamed The Devil because of his dark skin and hair. Geeraard and his wife are both buried in St Bavo's crypt.

The castle became a monastery in the sixteenth century and a seminary was installed in the grounds. Later it was transformed into a school, then a lunatic asylum, and then an orphanage. At the moment it holds the city archives and the only part open to the public is the reading room, which is a shame.

The Seminary

The building opposite the castle was originally built as a seminary. It opened its doors in 1914, just in time for the German army to walk in and take it over as a barracks. At the end of the war the Belgian army moved in and continued to use it as a barracks.

It wasn't until 1927 that it finally became a seminary as originally intended. It then closed in 2002 and is now the Vlerick business School, where students study surrounded by the original stained glass windows and religious statuary.

Map 4.4 - Continue along the waterside. Just before you reach the bridge you will see a white building on your right. That was the Hotel Van Eersel.

Hotel van Eersel

This building was constructed in the eighteenth century by another Geeraard, Govaert Geeraard van Eersel, a priest from Antwerp.

It is now the main entrance of Sint Bavohumaniora, a secondary school for girls which was founded by the Sisters of Charity between WWI and WWII. It was the first Flemish speaking school for girls in Ghent, and it's only since 2013 that the school has accepted boys. You might see the pupils in their green uniforms.

Map 4.5 - When you reach the bridge turn left to cross it.

Ahead of you is the gleaming white Bishop's Palace which stands on what was once the Cathedral cemetery. Walk towards the Palace.

Map 4.6 - You will see two streets running down each side of the Bishop's Palace. Take the right-hand street, Hoofdkerkstraat.

At its end turn left into Kapittelstraat. It will almost immediately swing sharply right and take you towards the back of the cathedral.

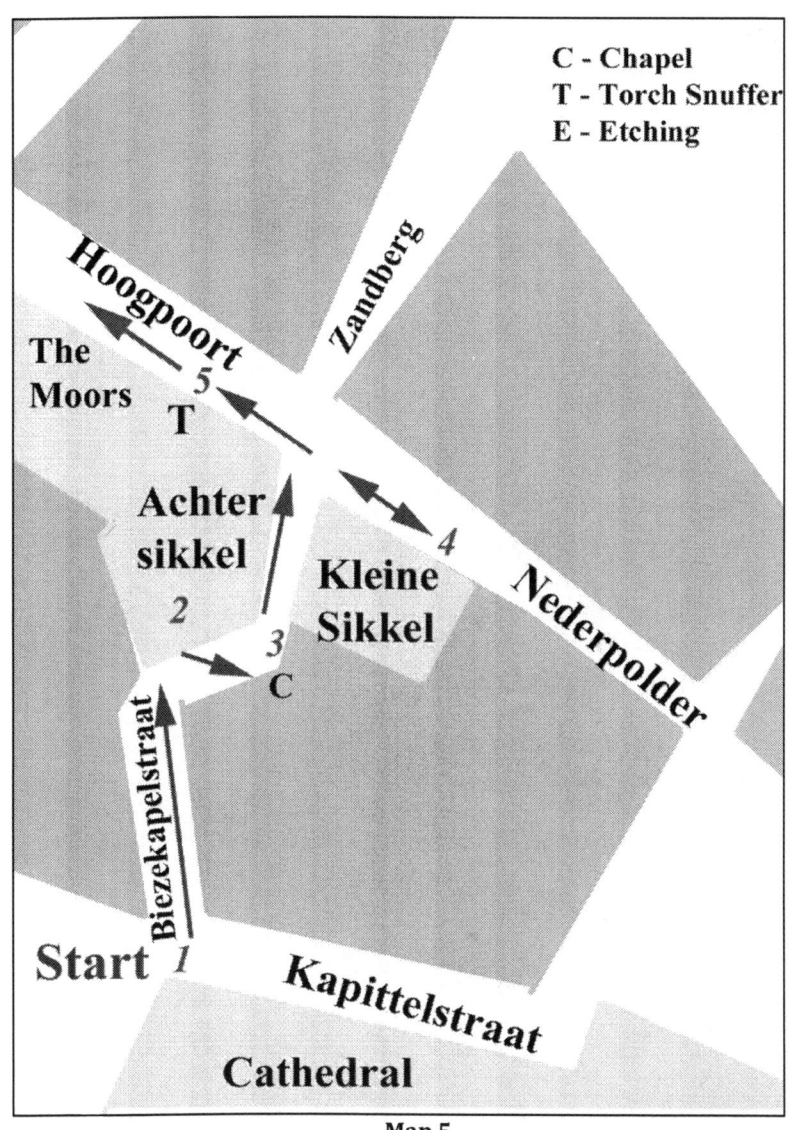

Map 5

Map 5.1 – As you approach the end of the Cathedral, turn right down Biezekapelstraat.

Follow this quiet little street and you will reach an old building complex known as the Achtersikkel on your left.

Achtersikkel

The inner courtyard and its surrounding buildings used to belong to the very wealthy Vander Sickelen family. They were one of the oldest families in Ghent, and closely involved in the politics and governing of Ghent.

A hint on how wealthy and powerful that family was is the fact that their courtyard has its very own well. A well was a rare and precious commodity in the Middle Ages, in fact Ghent had only five wells for the entire population.

The white limestone tower with its octagonal belfry stands out from the surrounding buildings which now house Ghent's Academy of Music. It's a shame you can't actually go inside the tower, but you might be lucky and stumble on a free concert in the courtyard. You will probably hear someone practicing some sort of music in the background.

Map 5.2 - Leave the Achtersikkel courtyard. Turn left to continue along Biezekapelstraat.

Just a few steps will bring you to the little Biezekapelletje on your right.

Biezekapelletje

This is a little chapel containing a statue of the Virgin Mary. The current statue is quite recent as it's only from the twentieth century, but the chapel is much older.

It was built in the seventeenth century and like many little chapels it has a legend. A passing soldier mocked the statue of the Virgin Mary and fired his gun at it. He should have known better – the bullet ricocheted off the statue, hit the soldier, and killed him.

Later during the French occupation, the statue was removed and the chapel was bricked up. It lay hidden until 1931 when restoration started and the Sisters of Charity took the little chapel under their wing.

Map 5.3 - Continue along Biezekapelstraat and at its end you will reach a crossroads. Turn right into Nederpolder.

De Kleine Sikkel

The first building on your right is called de Kleine Sikkel. It was also owned by the Vander Sickelen family.

This building was really quite derelict until 2018 when Ghent decided to save it and restoration began. Hopefully when you reach it the works will be complete.

Look above the second window on Nederplder to see the Vander Sickelen family coat of arms - with its three sickles representing the family name.

Map 5.4 - Backtrack to the junction and walk straight ahead into Hoogpoort.

Hoogpoort

This is one of the oldest streets in Ghent. It connects Ghent's two rivers, the Leie and the Scheldt. As you walk along it you will reach the front of the Achtersikkel on your left.

Spot the antique torch snuffer still attached to the wall by the door at number 64. In mediaeval times horsemen had to carry torches to find their way around towns as there was no such thing as public lighting. Visitors to the Sickelen family would snuff their torches out here before entering the premises.

Map 5.5 – Just beyond the Achtersikkel building you will reach the first of two high step-gabled buildings.

The Moors

They were also owned by the Sickelen family. There is a medieval carving on the first floor of each building; one is called De Witte Moor and the other De Zwarte Moor, The White Moor and the Dark Moor. They represent the lighter and darker stone used in building the two houses.

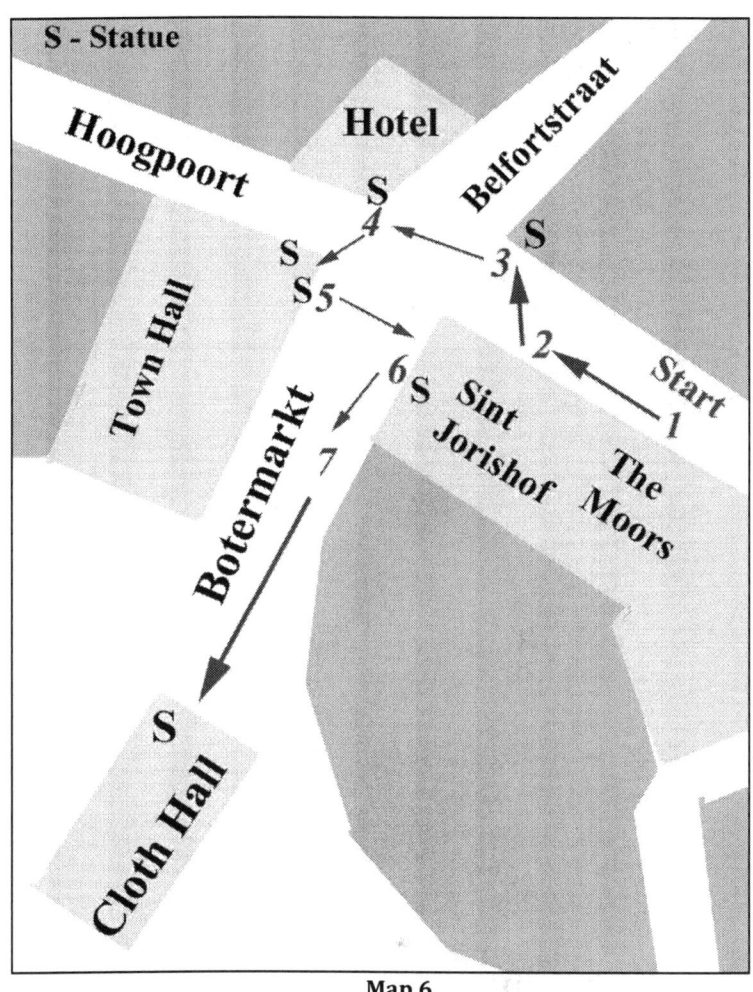

Map 6

Map 6.1 – Next door to the Dark Moor is what used to be the Guild Hall of Saint George, known as Sint Jorishof.

The Guild of Saint George

This was the Guild Hall of the Crossbowmen. As you walk along you will see the coats of arms of the guildsmen on the side of the building.

The guild is recorded as taking part in the Crusades in the eleventh century, travelling to Constantinople and Jerusalem to defend the "Holy Land". The Crossbowmen were a very powerful guild, entrusted with defending the city. They were so highly regarded that they led parades and public ceremonies in Ghent

Appropriately their guildhall stands in what was the political and economic centre of town. In the town archives, a law which supports the importance of the guild states:

> Nobody is allowed, noble or not,
> to carry or walk before the banner of Saint George,
> the banner of Flanders and the town of Ghent"

St Jorishof Hotel

Their guild hall became the St Jorishof Hotel in 1288 and is one of the oldest hotels in Europe.

Its most famous resident was Maria Countess of Burgundy, who signed the "Groot Privilege" (Great Privilege) in 1477. Maria was just twenty when she inherited Flanders from her father but was in danger of losing it through rebellion. So she negotiated and signed the Groot Privilege, which gave the Flemish cities their independence in exchange for staying under her reign. No doubt that precious document was kept in the Belfry Secure Room, under lock and key.

The hotel has had other famous visitors, including Napoleon who visited in 1805.

Map 6.2 - Continue to the crossroads but don't cross it yet!

On your right-hand side at the corner of Hoogpoort and Belfortstraat is a statue of Jacob van Artevelde.

Jacob van Artevelde

He was the head of the various Guilds in Ghent and he played a delicate balancing act during the Hundred Years War between England and France. He tried to keep Ghent and other Flemish towns neutral as they needed the vital English wool for the weaving trade.

However he eventually tried to have England's Black Prince proclaimed as the Count of Flanders. But that turned out to be a step too far. The Flemish population was enraged at the idea of an English Count of Flanders and there were riots. Jacob Artevelde was hacked to death during an uprising.

Map 6.3 - Opposite Jacob on the other side of Belfortstraat you will see a lovely building which is now a hotel. Cross Belfortstraat to reach it.

Philip van Artevelde

The hotel has a wonderful little turret which is guarded by a soldier - Philip van Artevelde, the son of Jacob van Artevelde.

Philip's fate is illustrated just around the corner on Belfortstraat. Look up to the first floor of the hotel and you will find a bas-relief of the battle of Roosebeke.

Battle of Roosebeke

That battle was fought between the Flemish army and the mighty army of France. Philip van Artevelde raised the Flemish army against the French, trying to support the English claim to the French crown.

Flanders lost that battle and Philip van Artevelde was killed - he is the dying soldier lying on the ground on the bas-relief. His body was strung up on a tree by the French for all to see.

Map 6.4 - Stand beneath the statue of Philip van Artevelde. Across Hoogpoort you will see the side of Ghent Town Hall.

Gothic Town Hall

Ghent built its first Town hall in 1482 - up to that point the powers-that-be had to meet in each other's homes. It only took 2 years to complete, but it was soon found to be too small to handle all of prosperous Ghent's business.

Ghent had a rethink and started building bigger and better in 1518. They constructed the section of the Town Hall which you can see in front of you, which is flamboyantly Gothic.

It is adorned with statues of Flemish Rulers from the past. The statues themselves are relatively modern - they were sculpted in the twentieth century but were made to look older.

On the corner of Hoogpoort and Bootermarkt where you are standing, you will find two famous ladies who ruled The Netherlands.

The family connections between the royal families of Europe in the Middle Ages were always intricate. The need for alliances and useful offspring from arranged marriages eventually resulted in swathes of Europe being ruled by one vast extended family. These two women were part of that family.

The lady facing you in Hoogport is Margaret of Austria.

Margaret of Austria

Margaret was Spanish and the daughter of the Holy Roman Emperor Maximilian I.

She eventually married Philibert II the Duke of Savoy but he died just three years later. Her brother, the crown prince, also died. So her father, Emperor Maximilian appointed Margaret as regent to her nephew Charles who was just five. She ruled The Netherlands successfully in his name until Charles came of age.

When he took the crown he became Charles V, The Holy Roman Emperor. At that point he sent his aunt into retirement. Just five years later he figured out that her advice and know-how were much too useful to lose, and reappointed her as ruler of The Netherlands.

Just round the corner, the lady on Botemarkt is Isabella of Portugal.

Isabella of Portugal

She was a princess of Portugal and married into the Hapsburg family. Her husband was Charles V, the Holy Roman Emperor, so she became queen of many countries at one fell stroke. She also became Duchess of Burgundy which at that time included The Netherlands.

Map 6.5 - With Isabella behind you, look across Botermarkt to the Coeur St George bistro.

Coeur St George bistro

Above the entrance is a quirky modern statue of Saint George. High above that is a much more traditional statue of St George on his horse killing the dragon.

Map 6.6 – Cross Botermarkt to reach the Bistro. Turn right to walk down Botermarkt and you will see a dramatic change in style in the two halves of the Town Hall.

Renaissance Town Hall

In 1540 Ghent decided to refuse to pay a new tax levied by Charles V, the Holy Roman Emperor. The city suffered the consequences and work on the Town Hall stopped and didn't start again until 1572.

As you see the Town Hall changes into a much more restrained Renaissance style. The change reflects the fashion of the two periods when the building was constructed. In fact it looks like two different buildings.

The new part of the Town Hall has a gorgeous stairway at the front. It was added for Napoleon's visit in the nineteenth century.

It's not possible to visit the Town Hall unless you organize a private guide through the tourist office – which might prove to be expensive. So you need to imagine the vaulted Arsenal Hall, the Wedding Chapel with its stained glass windows, and most intriguingly the Pacification hall with its black and white labyrinth embedded in the paving.

Map 6.7 - Continue down Botermarkt to reach the end of the Town Hall. In front of you stands the Cloth Hall and on your right you will see the Sheep-pen once more.

Walk 1 ends here.

If you want to explore more, you could join Walk 2 which starts just a few steps away. To reach it, just turn right to walk under the Sheep-pen to its far end.

Walk 2 – The Markets and the Castle

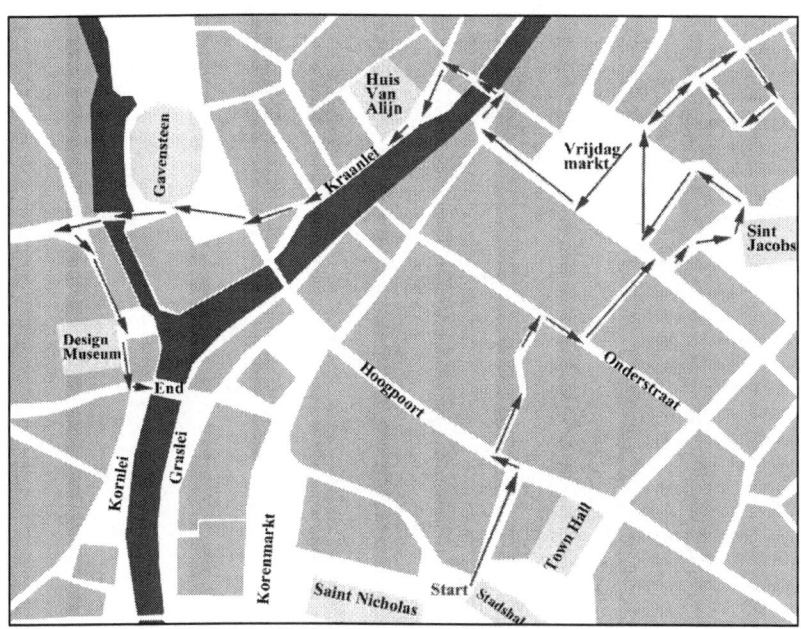

Walk 2 Overview

This walk starts in Goudenleeuwplein which lies near the back of Saint Nicholas' Church

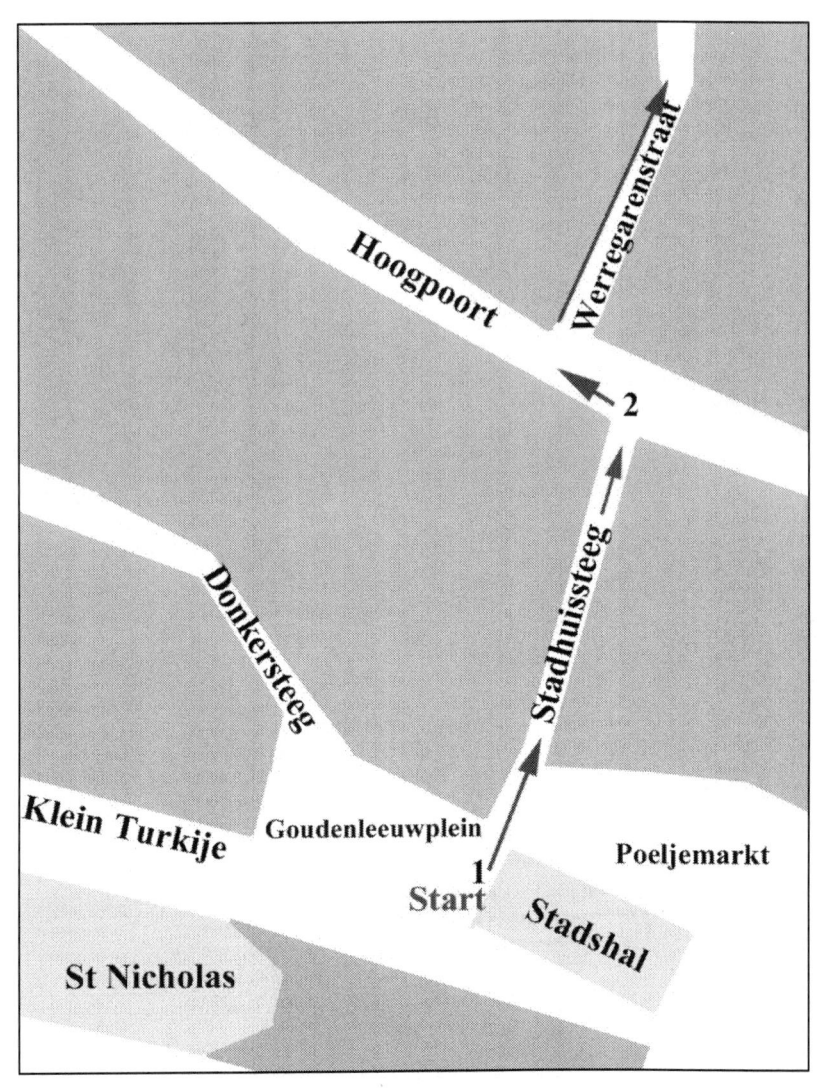

Map 1

Map 1.1 - Stand facing the west end of the "Sheep-pen" (Stadshal). Turn left to leave the square via Stadhuissteeg.

At the end of Stadhuissteeg you will reach a T-junction with Hoogpoort.

Map 1.2 – Take a few steps left into Hoogpoort, and then take the first right – it's just before number 37.

It's easy to miss this turning as it's a covered narrow entrance and it may look a bit uninviting at first – but persevere. This is Werregarenstraat, nicknamed Graffitistraat.

Graffitistraat

Ghent has two locations where graffiti is allowed and this is one of them. Every now and then Ghent whitewashes the walls to give the artists a new easel to work on.

The "artists" are always modifying the display and it's certainly colourful, however the quality of the art is variable. Sometimes all you will find is names splattered on all the walls, which is really quite boring. Hopefully the "good artists" will have been busy when you visit.

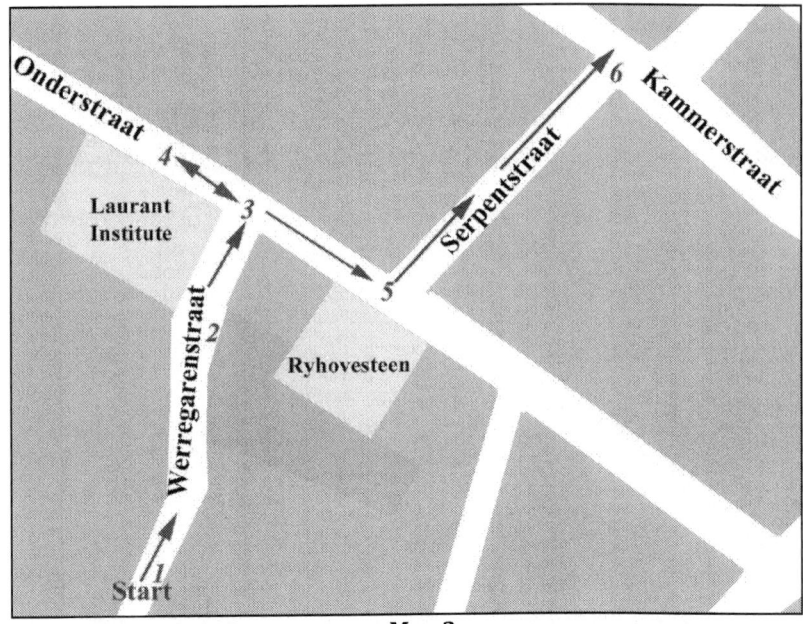

Map 2

Map 2.1 - As you walk along Graffiti Street you will come to a tiny park on your right-hand side.

Ryhovesteen

The park was originally a medieval vegetable garden and the "castle" which owned it is the stepped gable house which looks over the garden. It has a short arcade running along part of the ground floor.

It was called Ryhovesteen and was built in the twelfth century by the Kethulle family who were the Lords of Ryhove. It later became a prison for any Catholic clergy imprisoned during the protestant upheavals which sprung up all over the Low Countries.

Since then it's been used for various purposes and was even a brothel at one point. Nowadays it has regained respectability and is a public service building.

Map 2.2 - Exit Graffitistraat via another tunnel onto Onderstraat.

Map 2.3 - Cross Onderstraat and take a few steps to your left. Look up at the building which sits to the right of the tunnel you have just come through.

Laurent Institute

This building was originally called the Hof van Schardau. It was the home of Sir Van Der Gracht, lord of Schardau, who was also the bailiff of Ghent.

It was later bought by Ghent and turned into an orphanage for girls. The girls were called the Blauwe Meiskens, the Blue Girls, and they were taught various useful skills such as lacemaking.

They gained a reputation for fine work and the Blauwe Meiskens were awarded prizes for their lace at the World Exhibition in Paris in 1855.

Francois Laurent

By the late nineteenth century the building became a school. The school has "Institut Laurent" etched across the top of the façade, as it was named after Professor Francois Laurent.

He was one of the drivers of education for the working classes. His views on how society should take care of its citizens were very much against those held by the Catholic Church, which normally spells disaster for the person involved. However Laurent was an influential member of the Belgian government and he held onto his position and power.

The building is beautifully decorated, with a stepped gable, and little angels depicting ideal attributes such as order, discipline, education, courage and prosperity. There are also figures illustrating subjects which should be studied such as literature, sports, mathematics, and astronomy.

Map 2.4 - Backtrack along Onderstraat. Walk about 50 meters to reach the next street on your left which is cobbled Serpentstraat.

Before you go down it, take a look at the building on your right – it's the front of the Ryhovesteen which you read about in Grafitistraat and which sits in the little park.

Map 2.5 - Now walk into Serpentstraat.

Serpentstraat

This little street was a popular shopping area in the nineteenth century but it fell out of favour, businesses closed, and it lay abandoned.

Times change though and it is busy once more, appealing to anyone seeking something to wear which is a bit out of the ordinary. Have a look and something might catch your eye in the old wooden shop windows as you pass through.

Map 2.6 - At its end you will emerge into Kammerstraat.

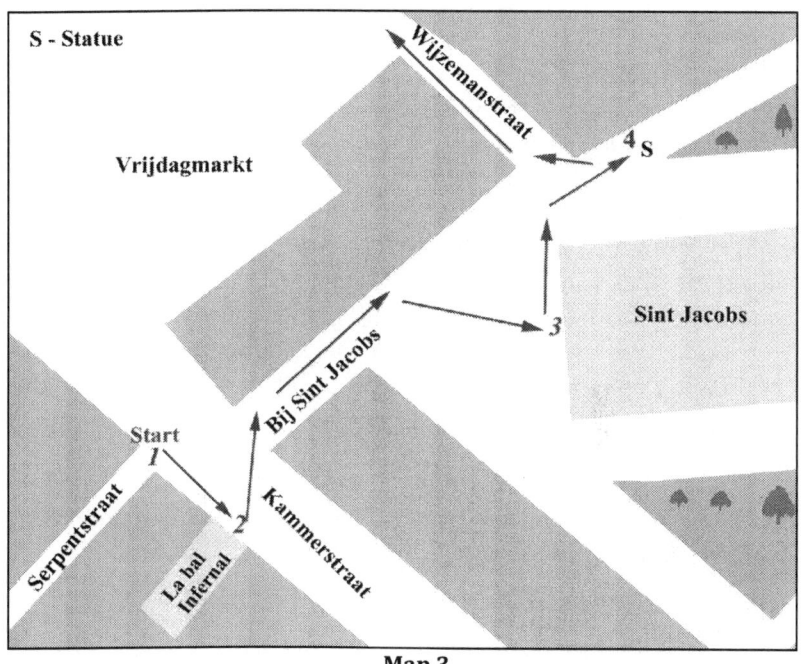

Map 3

Map 3.1 - You will see a large square on your left, but for now turn right to reach the third shop on your right at number 6

La bal Infernal

This is another chance for coffee if you haven't indulged yet. It's worth a look because it's a used-book café.

The walls are filled with used books and the idea is that you can either buy one you fancy, or swap one of your own old books for a small charge – at the time of writing it costs one Euro.

Map 3.2 - When you want to move on, cross Kammerstraat diagonally left from the front of the La Bal Infernal.

Walk into Bij Sint-Jacobs. Ahead of you stands Sint Jacobs's church, so make your way towards it.

Bij Sint-Jacobs

If you are here at the weekend you will find a flea market in the square, which can be fun to have a look round.

Sint Jacobs church

Way back in the eleventh century there was a little wooden chapel on this site. It was called Sint-Jacobs-in-de-meerschen, Saint James in the marshes, as this was a marshland long ago. The church was used by pilgrims on the St James Way to Santiago de Compostella in Spain. It's been rebuilt many times over the centuries, resulting in the church you see today.

The Church is beautiful and the oldest in Ghent, but It's only open from April to October in the afternoons, so you may find the doors shut. If not, do pop in.

Jan Palfijn

The church does not hold any famous works of art; however it does hold the tomb of Jan Palfijn. Not a name most people will recognize but he is someone who women should say a quiet thank-you to.

Peter Chamberlain was the English obstetrician to the British Royal Family – mostly because his family had invented a secret instrument to help with difficult births – forceps. However it was a secret they kept for about 150 years. Women outside the ranks of royalty and the aristocracy had to deliver without the doctor's help.

To keep their secret, the forceps were hidden in a lined box and only extracted once everyone was out the delivery room and the struggling mother was blindfolded.

Step up Jan Palfijn who heard rumors from England about this contraption, and reinvented it. The difference was that Palfijn did not want them kept a secret. He demonstrated his version in Paris, and soon forceps were being manufactured all over Europe and saving countless lives.

He died in poverty and he was buried in the church graveyard in the little corner reserved for the poor – now long gone. Years later Ghent decided that the city should also honour him and a monument was constructed. It has a grieving woman leaning on the tomb mourning his death.

Map 3.3 - When you exit the church face away from the church doors. Turn right to go round the corner of the church. You will see a carved pillar at the corner of Wijzemanstraat.

Totem Pole

The square around the church is the centre of the Ghent Folk Festival in mid-July. So it's appropriate that the odd totem pole statue just to the left of the church is located here.

It depicts the songs of Karel Waeri, a Ghent folk singer from the nineteenth century who was famous for singing in the Ghent dialect. He sang against poverty, exploitation, and capitalism but was also fond of very filthy explicit songs. The totem pole has ten figures depicting his favourite topics and songs.

You can have a listen to an old recording on this link:

https://www.youtube.com/watch?v=WfK8cgYk1BI

Map 3.4 - Stand near the totem pole, with both the church and the totem pole on your left. Take the first right into Wijzemanstraat and it will take you into Vrijdagmarkt.

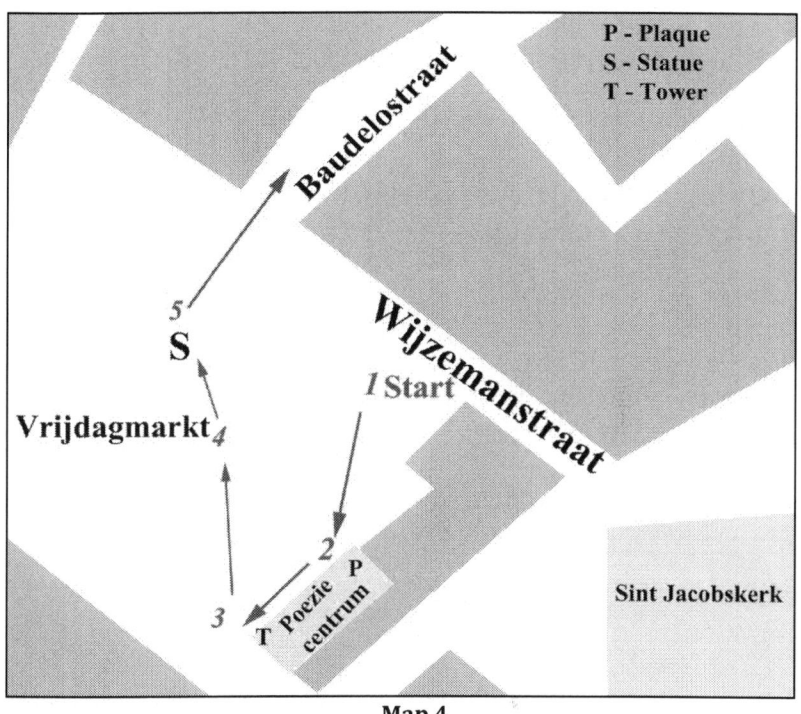

Map 4

Vrijdagmarkt

This is a very old square named after the market which started in 1199 and is still held here on Friday mornings. There is also a weekend market which on Sundays transforms into a bird market. It is a popular place to meet and socialize.

It's been a place of many important scenes in the history of Ghent. Many of the buildings around the square were Guild houses – now mostly turned into bars and restaurants.

Two of Ghent's most important guilds were the weavers and the fullers, and they were always vying for position and power. The weavers produced huge sheets of cloth. The fullers then treated the cloth to produce a valuable soft felt-like fabric – so both were very important trades.

However, in 1345 the weavers gained the upper hand politically. The rivalry between the two guilds erupted into a battle on this square and resulted in hundreds of deaths - the Weavers emerged as victors.

Just five years later trouble flared up on this square again, and once more hundreds died, but this time the Fullers were victorious. The Fullers took their revenge on the survivors; the weavers were fined, imprisoned, and forbidden to hold weapons or to gather in number.

Map 4.1 - Walk along the left hand side of the square towards the pretty white tower in front of you.

Paul Snoek

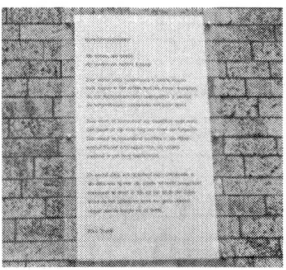

As you do, you will find a plaque on the wall on your left-hand side.

Ghent is very fond of poetry and you can find poems displayed in various locations as you explore. This one is in an appropriate spot, beside the Poëziecentrum, Ghent's Poetry Centre.

The poem is by Paul Snoek who was a Belgian poet from the last century. It is called Schildersverdriet, or Artist's Sorrow. The poet clearly doesn't believe that an artist has a happy life. It translates very loosely as:

> All stones, all cities
> are places of destruction & art.
>
> There, white artists live in black houses.
> There in the soft bed of the muses sleep virgins,
> who let their love membranes burst open at night
> like air mattresses pumped with better blood.
>
> There the artist dies his daily scary death.
> Then a tear of turpentine pearls from his red eye.
> Then he weeps inconspicuously softly into his ribs,
> from which he cannot escape, like fingers
> sweating in a hot glove.
>
> And because all that he loved is as imperfect
> as all that he has touched with his good will,
> he accepts to be sad until the end of time.
> Because after painting comes great sorrow,
> deeper than the emptiness after love.

Map 4.2 - Continue in the same direction to reach the corner of the Poëziecentrum.

Poëziecentrum (Poetry Centre)

The Poetry Centre is dedicated to poetry written in the Dutch language including Afrikaans.

The building is the oldest building on the Vrijdagmarkt. As you might expect it was once a guild house, the Tanners Guild in fact. Its tower is called the Toreken and it was restored in 1982.

The bell which had hung there from the sixteenth century was also restored – it had been languishing in the belfry museum for a hundred years. It used to ring out to announce the opening of the Friday Market.

Map 4.3 - Walk over towards the statue in the middle of the square. Turn round to look back at the Toreken about half way over.

Melusine

At the top of the tower is a pretty if rather two-dimensional weather vane – it's a mermaid gazing into a mirror.

Her name is Melusine, and she appears in many North European folk tales and legends. In fact several royal ancient royal families, e.g. The Plantagenets who ruled England in the Middle Ages, are said to be descended from Melusine.

Map 4.4 - Continue to the statue in the middle of the square.

Jacob Van Artevelde

This is Jacob Van Artevelde, "The Wise Man of Ghent" who you read about at the end of Walk 1. He is pointing towards England, the primary source of wool which made Ghent rich. As you know he came to an unfortunate end and it was not until 500 years later that a decision was made to honour him with this statue. Beneath him are four ladies who represent Ypres, Ghent, Bruges, and Flanders.

A Little Detour

The next part of this walk takes you into a little area where the houses are decorated with odd etchings and inscriptions. It's a pleasant walk but there are no major sights to see.

If time is tight or that does not appeal to you, continue this walk from "Exploring the rest of the square" on page 80.

Map 4.5 – To take the little detour, stand back to back with Jacob and walk straight ahead into Baudelostraat.

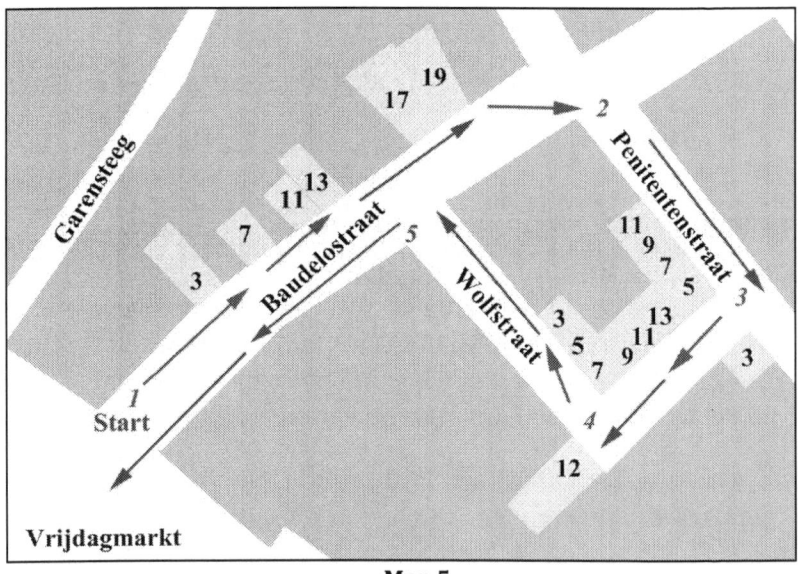

Map 5

Baudelostraat

This is one of Ghent's prettiest streets. It's lined with step-gabled houses, some with balconies, impressive bay windows, and lots of decoration.

Many of them were designed by Jacob Gustaaf Semeij who came from Ghent. He was an ardent supporter of all things Flemish and part of the Flemish National Party. He liked to add very individual Flemish touches to his creations.

Map 5.1 - Here are some to hunt down as you walk along it.

Chickens

Number 3 on the left-hand side is decorated with a cockerel and a hen facing each other on either side of the large bay window.

The Sunflower

Spot the sunflower at number 7 on your left. It's just past the entrance to the underground carpark. The inscription above the window translates (roughly) as:

| If ye praise |
| with flower or green |
| that's the foreplay |
| from a kiss |

Adam and Eve House

Number 11 is known as the "Adam and Eve House" and it's easy to see why. On the beautiful carving, Eve is handing Adam the fateful apple.

The House of the Burning Candle

Number 13 has an inscription on either side of the balcony which sounds like a riddle:

> I consume myself
> to enlighten others

It's encouraging us to always help our fellow citizens.

The Construction Workshop

Number 15 just next door has two engravings displaying the tools of the building trade. Between them it says:

> Charpentes Metalliques

which translates as "Steel Structures".

It now houses the Antiq Depot and if you venture inside you will find a huge collection of "antiques" small and large on sale. If you love old things it's worth a look around.

Huis de Druivelaar

Number 17 is the Huis de Druivelaar and it has bunches of grapes at the side of the large window. The inscription reads:

> The best grain is there
> in the middle of the sheaf
> the ripest grape
> shuffles in the closest foliage

It seems to be saying that you must look for the good things as they are hidden.

Baudeloo House

At number 19 we find the monks who were installed in the nearby Baudelo Abbey. The Baudelokapel still stands just a few streets away. Mozart played the organ in the chapel on a tour of the Low Countries in 1765.

The monasteries in Flanders were dissolved not long after that and the Baudelokapel was later turned into the University library. These days it's an events location for everything from weddings to seminars.

Map 5.2 - When you reach the crossroads turn right into Penitentenstraat.

Penitentenstraat

The next few houses all have little mottos on them – all telling us to live a good and productive life. Find the houses below which are all on your right-hand side and look below their windows to find the etchings.

Number 11

He who cares on time shows wise policy

Number 9

> Battle gives life

Number 7

> Who lives life uselessly
> leads a plant life

Number 5

Number 5 sits on the corner of Wolfstraat. Its motto is split around the base of three windows of the house.

> There is only one happiness, the duty
> One consolation, the labor
> One pleasure, the beauty

Number 3

On the corner of Wolfstraat you will find a building with some beautiful painted floral decoration above the windows.

Map 5.3 – Now turn right into Wolfstraat.

Wolfstraat

This street is full of yet more good advice and odd carvings.

Number 13

This house is known as The Sturgeon because of the large fish and seahorse engraved below the window.

Number 11

Just next door is more worthy advice.

> Toon wat gij kunt doen
> men zal u zeggen wie gij zijt
>
> Show what you can do,
> they will tell you who you are

Number 9

Here is a lovely carving of a wolf and cubs on the move. If you look up you will see Romulus and Remus suckling the she-wolf from Roman legend. Perhaps this house is where the street gets its name from.

Number 12 - Huis de Passer

Number 12 on the corner was the home of architect Semeij himself, and it is called Huis de Passer. You can see Semeij's name carved on the upper façade

It's a beautiful art deco building. At the top you can see a figure and some cherubs designing a building. Lower down is an engraving of the builder's tools.

Semeij was an ardent member of the Flemish Nationalist Party which fell out of favour with the government in 1918. He had to leave the country and at that point his lovely house was plundered by his political enemies. He was allowed to return to Ghent in 1929.

On the façade you can find another helpful saying:

> Wie taal en kunsten mint,
> mint volk en vaderland
>
> Who loves Language and arts
> loves people and country

Map 5.4 - Follow Wolfstraat around the corner.

Number 7

The house on the corner gives us some more wise words:

> Leg water honderd jaar op vaten, 't wordt toch nooit geen wijn
>
> Put water in barrels for a hundred years, it never becomes wine

Number 5

This one's motto is a bit sexist:

> 't Naaikussen is der vrouwe lessenaar
>
> The sewing pad is the lady's desk

Number 3

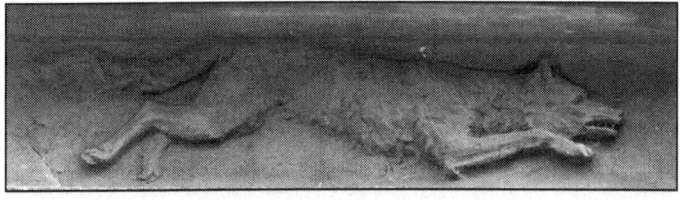

And finally you see another Wolf at number 3.

Map 5.5 - When you reach Baudelostraat, turn left to return to Vridgemarkt. Once there walk over to the statue of Jacob Van Artevelde in the middle of the square once more.

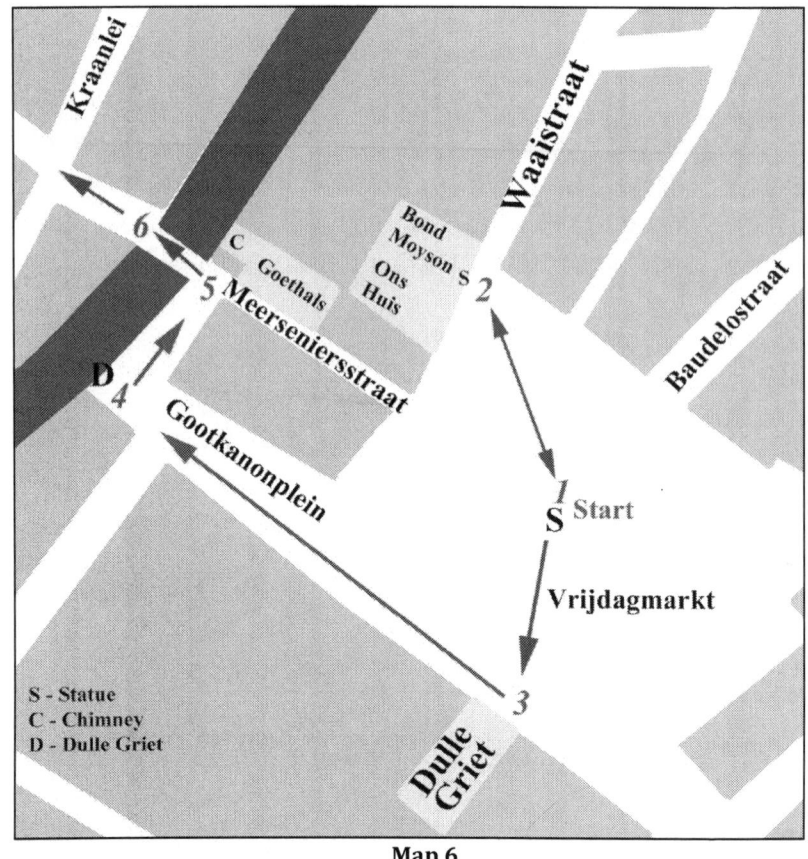

Map 6

Exploring the rest of the square

Map 6.1 – Stand back to back with Jacob and look diagonally left to find the Bond Moyson building – it's a bit of a give-away because it's written in big red letters across the top. Make your way over to it.

Bond Moyson and Ons Huis (Our House)

Next door to Bond Moyson stands Ons Huis. These two buildings were built in the twentieth century in the Art Deco style with a striking iron arch and glasswork. When they were built, the socialist movement had just started in Europe and trade unions came into being in Ghent. These buildi several socialist institutions including the first Co-operative which was started by the socialists to provide the essentials c to the people at a reasonable cost.

Spot the cockerel lifting his head to crow on the Bond Moyson building. He represents the wake-up of the people to a better life where everyone is equal.

The buildings used to have a lovely interior as well, but they are used as office space now and have lost most of the decoration. They are still linked to the socialist movement though, as they house various public services.

Map 6.2 - Return to the statue of Jacob Artevelde in the middle of the square. Now face the same direction as he does. Cross the road ahead of you to reach a pub called Dulle Griet (Mad Meg).

Dulle Griet Pub

It's a good pub to visit if you feel like a glass of beer; they have hundreds of different types.

If you are very brave you could try the Kwak yard beer in its special glass, however to make sure you don't pinch the glass, you have to pass over one of you shoes as a deposit. Your shoe will be put in a basket which is then hoisted high above the bar, and stays there until you return your glass.

Map 6.3 - When you exit the pub, face the square again and turn left to walk along the square's edge and leave it by walking straight into Grootkannonplein (Big Gun Square).

It will take you down to the riverside where you will find another Dulle Griet.

Dulle Griet

This huge iron cannon weighs in at over twelve tons. It was supposedly an early "super weapon", however it cracked the first time it was used and was never fired again.

It has always been red in colour and its other nickname was Rode Duyvele, Flemish for Red Devil.

Its mouth has been sealed up to stop people sticking all sorts of rubbish down it.

Map 6.4 - Face the river and turn right to continue along Grootkannonplein to reach the bridge.

Goethals Steam Mill and bakery

At the bridge you will find a very old bakery on Meerseniersstraat.

It has some lovely elderly carvings on the first floor. They show a horse, a mill, and a bakery, because this building was originally also a steam mill, vital to grind grain into flour.

The original miller was named Goethals and the same family was milling grain here until just 2008. Nowadays only the bakery survives.

Map 6.5 - Walk out to the middle of the bridge.

Zuivelbrug

The first wooden bridge on this spot was built in the thirteenth century. It has been rebuilt more than once, but in the eighteenth century it was replaced by a swing bridge to let larger boats pass through. That bridge was restored and made operable again in 1987.

Look to your right - you will see the high brick chimney which was part of the Goethals steam mill. In the other direction you get a nice shot of Dulle Griet.

Map 6.6 - Continue over the bridge and straight ahead into Kraanlei.

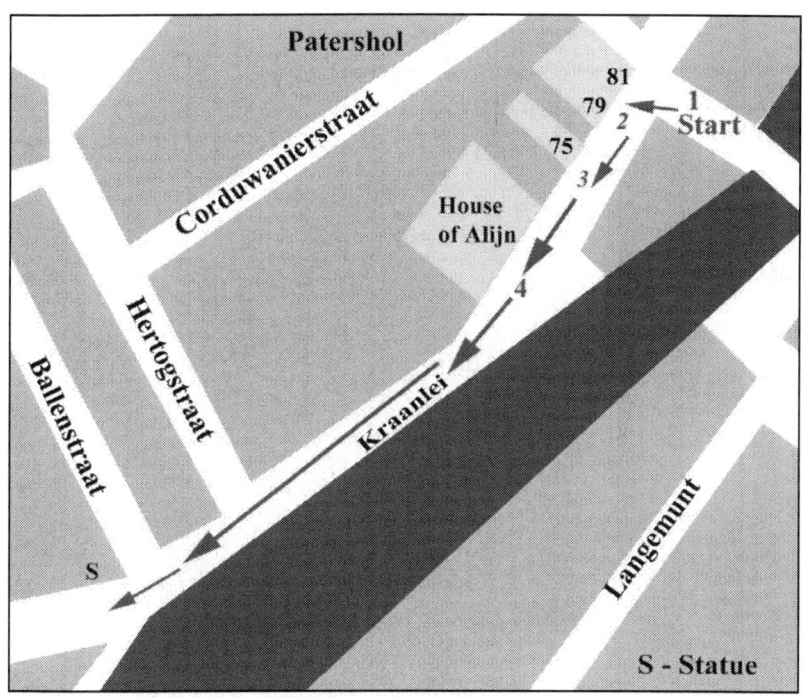

Map 7

Patershol district

Take note of where you are right now. If you were to go down Rodekoningstraat which is just ahead of you, you would be in the Patershol district – a very old part of Ghent full of little lanes and alleys.

Long ago Patershol was an affluent area, but with industrialization it became the home of labourers, and by the nineteenth century it had become a very deprived area. In fact Rodekoningstraat was a red-light district up to the Second World War.

Since then it has become a fashionable place to live once more, and it's full of interesting bars and restaurants – so worth a wander round in the evening.

Map 7.1 - For now though you will explore Kraanlei and its old step-gable houses. Just like those in Wolfstraat, they want to instruct us on how to be a better person. In front of you stands number 81.

Kraanlei 81 - The Flute Player

This is a lovely old house decorated with panels which illustrate the five senses, sight, touch, smell, hearing, and taste. Hearing is particularly lovely showing us a lady playing her instrument.

Almost right at the top of the building is the flute player which the building gets its name from.

Kraanlei 79

Just next door on the left is number 79 - it is decorated with panels illustrating six of the seven acts of mercy. It was inspired by "The Seven Acts of Mercy", a painting by Caravaggio, and those the stonemason illustrated were:

> Bury the dead
> Visit the imprisoned
> Visit the sick
> Feed the hungry
> Clothe the naked
> Refresh the thirsty

The missing seventh act is Shelter the Homeless, but perhaps the stonemason omitted that one as the building used to be an Inn, so giving shelter was what they did anyway? See if you can identify which engraving is which.

The building now houses an old fashioned sweetshop called Temmerman's which is worth a look in the window. Tourists are always encouraged to try Cuberdons, a local specialty, but be warned they are very, very sweet. If you would rather try something less sweet, try the really sour smoeletrekkers.

Map 7.2 – Facing number 79 turn left and walk just two doors down to reach number 75.

Kraanlei 75 - The Klok

This house is decorated with the cardinal virtues of bravery, prudence, justice and moderation, as well as love, hope and faith. The name of the house Klok means bell and it refers to the bell you can see just above the front door.

Map 7.3 - Face the Klok and turn left to continue along Kraanlei to reach the water side.

Kraanlei

This lovely old street gets its name from the crane which used to stand near here at the water's edge. It was used to unload cargo from the boats. Only small men were able to actually get in the crane to work it, and they were nicknamed the Kraankinders or "crane children".

On your right you will find the House of Alijn at number 65.

The House of Alijn

The buildings of this little museum were built as an act of contrition by the aristocratic Rijm family.

A beautiful girl named Godelieve was ordered by her father to marry wealthy Simon Rijm. However Godelieve fell in love with Hendrik Alijn and refused to comply with her father's order. Simon Rijm took the simplest way to get rid of his rival by killing both Hendrik and his brother Zeger. Simon's family connections and influence ensured that he escaped execution, although the family was exiled from Ghent.

After some years the exiles asked if they could return to Ghent. They were allowed to do so if they financed this establishment, which was to be used to house elderly women who had no means of support.

Nowadays the museum presents the little houses as different establishments, all furnished with everyday items from centuries ago – e.g. a classroom. It's perhaps of limited interest to a lot of visitors, but if you have the City Card and the time, the museum is probably worth a meander round.

However, even if you decide not to go into the museum itself, step inside just to see the courtyard, where you can partake of tea and cake.

Map 7.4 - Continue down Kraanlei passing Hertogstraat and Ballenstraat on your right.

As the road swings slightly away from the river, look for Ghent's own version of the more famous Mannekin Pis from Brussels - it's on your right-hand side.

Lena, Luna, and Nestor

The locals insist the little statue in the middle is actually older than the Mannekin Pis in Brussels. He is called Nestor and the girls on either side are Lena and Luna - the girls were added much more recently.

There is a theory that Nestor was put there to symbolize the urine purchased by the Tanners guild. They used it to soften and breakdown leather hides and made it easier for the tanners to remove hair and flesh from the hides.

Just like the Mannekin Pis, all three statues are often put into colourful outfits to celebrate special holidays and anniversaries. Recently they have donned full protective gear to lead the fight against Covid.

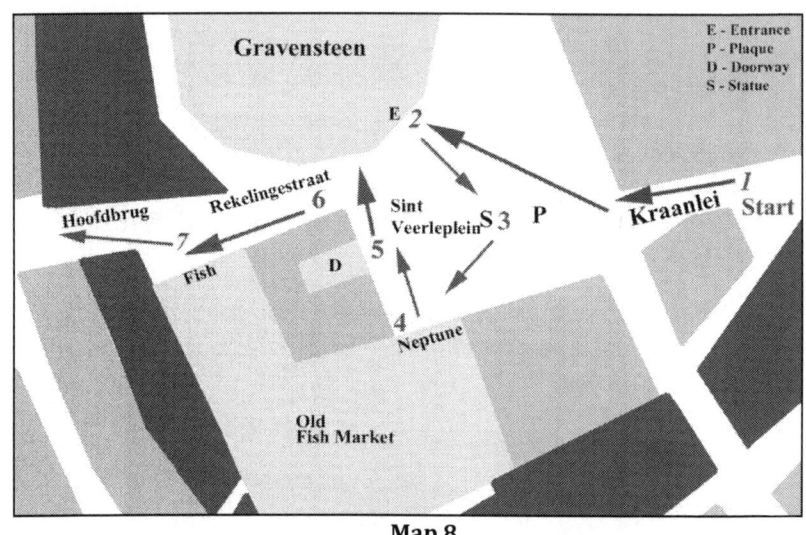

Map 8

Map 8.1 - Follow Kraanlei and you will soon walk into a little square called Sint Veerleplien. On the right you will find Gravensteen (the castle) so walk towards it. Watch out for the trams as you do!

Castle of the Counts

This is the Castle of the Counts. The Counts were of course the Counts of Flanders who ruled for centuries.

Look above the entrance to find a Latin inscription stating that it was built in 1180 by Count Philip of Alsace.

Above that you can see an odd cross shaped window, which was put there to celebrate the fact that Count Philip had just returned from a Crusade which seems very commendable. Less commendable, the castle's main purpose was to intimidate Ghent's population and let them know who was boss.

As you might guess by looking at it, the castle wasn't the most comfortable of residences. So by the fourteenth century the Counts had moved to a much more desirable property further from the centre of town, and they just used this enormous pile of stone for official receptions.

Later the castle became a prison and a place of dread as horrible punishments were meted out; floggings, beheadings, and probably the most gruesome of all, burning at the stake. Its reputation hit an all-time low when the dreaded Spanish Inquisition took up residence, and dispensed its own brand of justice.

You can go inside and explore the dungeons and enjoy the views over the town. At the time of writing, the entrance ticket includes an audio guide; it's unusual in that it is actually funny, as Walter tells you his opinions and stories from the castle's history. Don't miss picking it up in the gift shop.

Map 8.2 - Back outside, face away from the castle. Find a colorful statue of a lion in the middle of Sint-Veerleplein, the little square in front of you.

Sint-Veerleplein
The lion marks the spot where terrible punishments took place. This is where counterfeiters were executed in a particularly gruesome way. They were thrown into a cauldron of boiling oil or water.

On a much happier note, the square also houses the art-work called

> Ai Natti Oggi
>
> Of Whom is Born Today

The lights around the square flash gently whenever a baby is born. The four Ghent hospitals are connected to the square so they can throw the switch when a baby arrives.

There is stone on the plaque which explains how it works. If you stand face to face with the lion, you will find it on the ground on your left-hand side.

It tells us:

> The Street lights on Sint-Veerleplein are connected to the maternity hospitals in the City of Ghent. Every time the light slowly flashes a child is born. This work is dedicated to the newborn and to all children who are born today in this city.

Map 8.3 – Make your way over to the corner behind the lion statue. You will find the entrance to the old Fish Market with its very striking doorway.

Old Fish Market

It's topped by Neptune and flanked by the rivers Scheldt and Leie, Ghent's two rivers. The man on the left represents the Leie and is holding a sail, whereas the women on the right represents the Scheldt and has a catch of fish.

The doorway originally had three sea gods but only Neptune survived a fire in 1874. It's no longer a fish market; in fact you will find the tourist office inside.

Map 8.4 - Stand so that the Fish Market doorway is behind you.

Walk along the left-hand side of the square to find the gateway of the Wenemaersgodshuis – it has a monk standing above the doorway.

Wenemaersgodshuis

A building and land was purchased on this spot in the fourteenth century by Willem Wenemaer who turned it into a godshuis for very poor elderly women from Ghent. Each resident had her own little house and garden, and most kept themselves by knitting and sewing and selling the results.

Since that time, the godshuis has been squabbled over by family descendants and the appointed guardians of the godshuis, leading to a yearly settling of accounts. Traditionally the annual meeting ended with a meal, but in the sixteenth century so many family descendants turned up for the meal that the guardians had to put a limit on how many could attend. The family was restricted to twelve representatives.

By the nineteenth century the building was very dilapidated, and when it was inspected by officials it was deemed not fit for purpose anymore. It closed in 1866 and the Fish Market gobbled up its land. All that is left now is this ornate doorway which is guarded by Saint Laurentius.

Map 8.5 - Face the castle and walk to the end of the square. Turn left to leave the square by Rekelingestraat.

Map 8.6 – Once you reach the water side on your right take a look at the building on your left. It is decorated with various fish, lobsters, and eels.

Map 8.7 - Walk onto the bridge, the Hoofdbrug.

Hoofdbrug

This bridge was also called the Execution Bridge. Until 1585 criminals such as murderers or rapists were decapitated on the stone bridge which once stood here. Of course there is a legend:

A father and son rebelled against the Count and were taken to the bridge to be executed. The Count decided to use the occasion to experiment in a bit of psychology. He wanted to find out if parents loved their children more than children loved their parents. He gave them the chance of freedom if either would decapitate the other. The father convinced his son to take the offer, as he had more life to live. The son was about to execute his father with the sword high above his head ready to swing down, when the sword fell to pieces. The Count decided to take this as a hint from God and pardoned them both.

If you go on one of the boat trips, the tour guide should point out a tiny little grill beneath the bridge. That is the window of the prison cell for the condemned, which is so small that the prisoners had to kneel while in it.

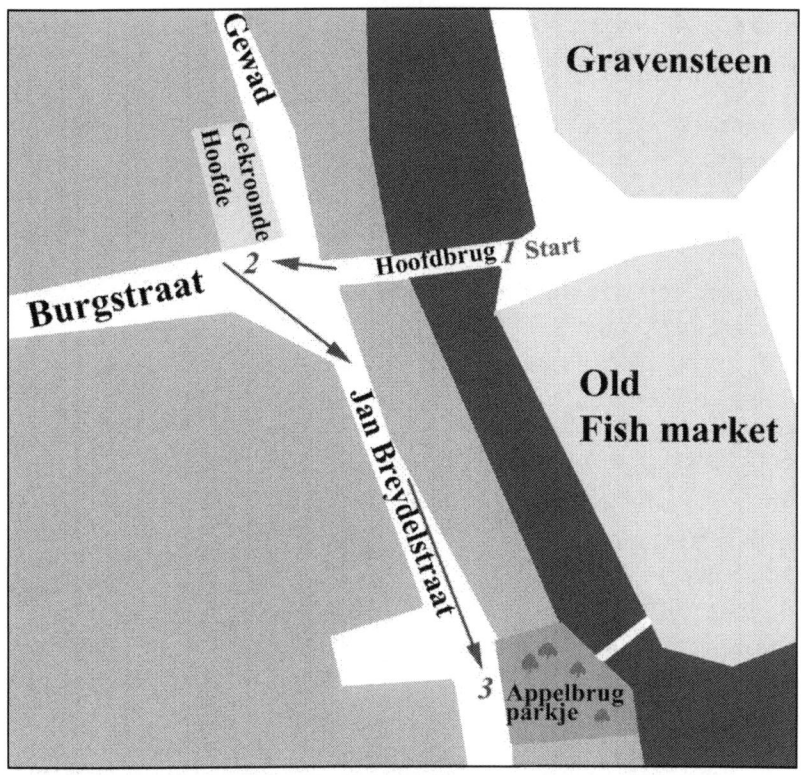

Map 9

Map 9.1 - Cross over the bridge, passing Gewad on your right. Pause at the first building after Gewad.

You are now on Burgstraat – this was once a very important street which led straight to the castle.

De GekroondeHoofde

The name means "The crowned heads". Look up to see the faces of many of the Flemish Counts staring down at you.

The Family tree of the Flemish ruling family is very, very complicated. The Flemish rulers basically expanded Flanders by marrying the heiresses of neighbouring lands, only to suffer the same fate, when Countess Margaret III of Flanders married the Duke of Burgundy.

From that point the country was ruled by France. It was then inherited by Austria, then by Spain, until it reunited with France after the French Revolution. This building shows the rulers in chronological order, from top to bottom and left to right.

Baldwin Emperor of Constantinople
William of Dampierre
Guy of Dampierre
Robert of Bethune
Louis of Nevers
Louis of Male
Philip the bold
John the Fearless
Philip the Good
Charles the Bold
Maximillian of Austria
Philip the Fair
Charles V Holy Roman Emperor
Philip II

Map 9.2 - Leave this history lesson behind. Face away from De GekroondeHoofde and walk straight ahead into Jan Breydelstraat towards the river.

Jan Breydelstraat
This little narrow street is full of interesting antique and bric-a-brac shops.

Map 9.3 - Don't miss a little square on your right; it's just beyond number 13. It is home to the most picturesque part of the Gravensteen Hotel. Just opposite it is a tiny park called the Appelbrugparkje.

Appelbrugparkje

It has a new glass-fibre bridge which goes straight into the old Fish market. The park has a nice view of the river and the Butchers Hall so you might want to pause for a little rest.

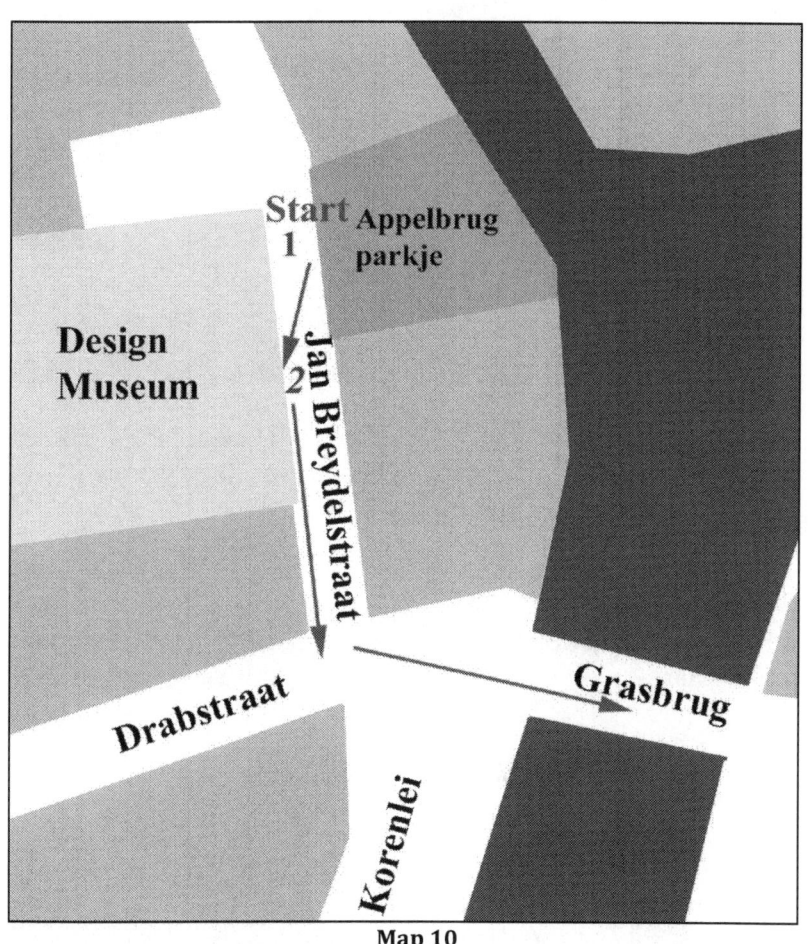

Map 10

Map 10.1 – Continue along Jan Breydelstraat. On the right hand side you will find the Design Museum in a huge old mansion.

Design Museum

The museum is in what was the old Hotel de Coninck. Even if you don't visit the museum itself, pop into the courtyard and admire the huge vase decorating the garden.

The museum has a split personality; the first part shows how the very, very wealthy lived long ago, but the new extension attached to the old building displays "interesting" Art Nouveau items that Ghent had squirreled away since the sixties and seventies.

The curators have sprinkled some items from the modern collection into the original old building which gives a jarring contrast.

The new extension has an ingenious interior with floors which can be reconfigured to the museum's designer's whim. A lot of the items on show epitomize the styles of the sixties and seventies and might make you smile – lava lamps!

Map 10.2 – *With the museum behind you turn right to walk down to the river. Turn left to walk onto the bridge. You have now reached the Grasbrug where this walk ends.*

You could continue with walk 3 which starts from the same point. Alternatively, walk over the bridge to find a café and some well-earned refreshments.

Walk 3 - Along the Canals

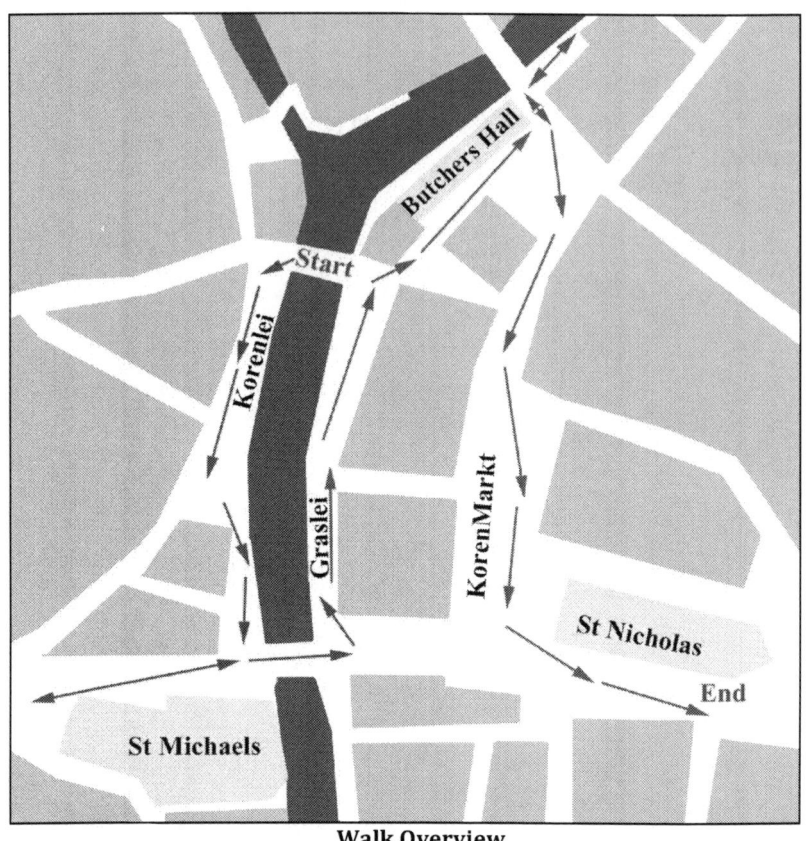

Walk Overview

This walk starts on the Grasbrug, a bridge which lies between Graslei and Korenlei.

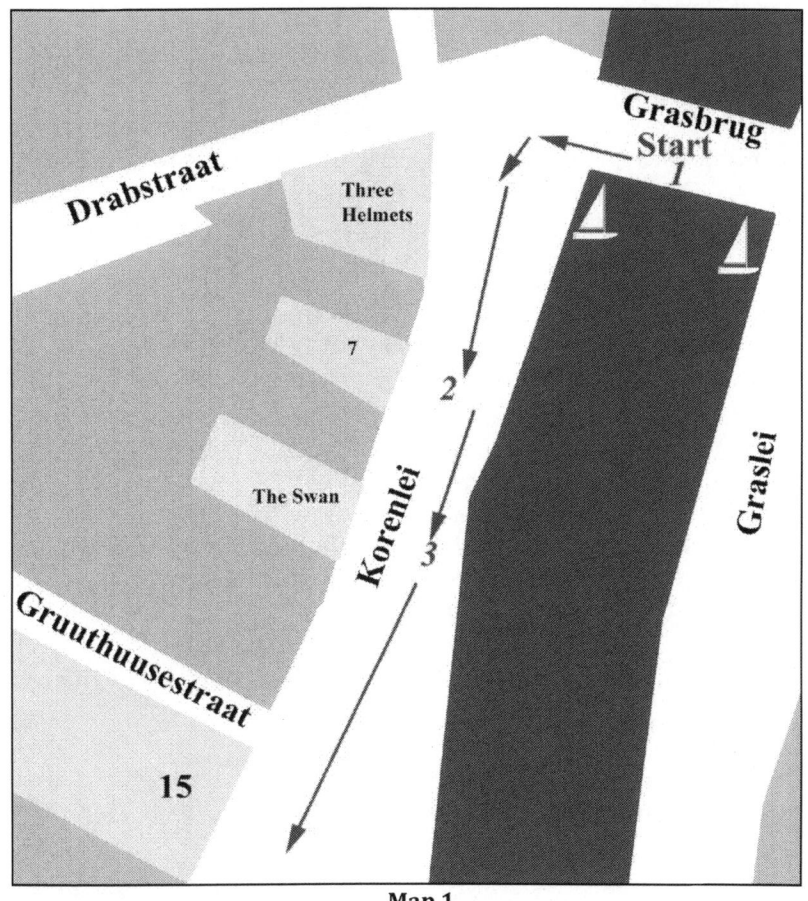

Map 1

From the bridge you will see a couple of boat departure points.

Boat trip

You will be encouraged to take a trip by the boat companies moored there. If you have purchased the Ghent City card, make sure you join a boat company which is included in that deal – there is no point in paying twice.

It's a nice trip on a sunny day and takes about forty minutes - the boats all take you along the same three stretches of water.

One of the crew will give a commentary on what you can see in multiple languages, including English. You might notice that the Flemish commentary lasts considerably longer than other languages.

Rabot and Stroppendrager

One of the stretches of water you will visit runs along to Rabot, one of Ghent's defenses. En route you will see all that's left of Charles V's palace and a statue of a Stroppendrager – those leaders of Ghent's failed rebellion who had to march to the castle with a noose around their necks.

Once back on dry land, re-orientate yourself by standing on the Grasbrug again and find Little Ben peeping over the buildings on your left hand side.

The road running down the right-hand side of the river is called Korenlei.

One of Ghent's most important privileges, was the edict that all grain imported into Flanders had to go through Ghent where it was taxed.

This area was where all the financial business was done, and as a result these impressive and beautiful buildings went up on both sides of the river.

As you walk along Korenlei, you will get a wonderful view of the lovely buildings on Graslei on the other side of the river. It's worth returning here in the evening to see the buildings all lit up - Ghent was awarded three stars by Michelin for its beautiful lighting scheme

Korenlei 5 - Five Helmets

The first building on Korenlei is number 5 where the old "Five Helmets" brewery once stood. It was later replaced by this building designed by local architect David 't Kindt.

From the bridge you should be able to spot a blue armillary globe right at the top of the building. However at the time of writing it is missing, assumed to be in restoration.

'T Kindt was very fond of armillary globes, so if you find others while exploring, the architect was probably 't Kindt.

Map 1.1 - Leave the bridge via the right-hand bank. Once over turn left to walk down Korenlei. Stop at number 7, two doors down from number 5.

Korenlei 7 – Gildehuis der Onvrije Schippers

This was the guild house of the unfree bargemen, and is easy to spot by the golden boat weather vane at the top. You need to stand back a bit to see it.

The building facade is decorated with lions, dolphins, scrolls, and a huge vase.

So who were the unfree bargemen? Quite simply they were transporters who had to unload their cargoes outside Ghent, and pay to have their merchandise transported into Ghent by the free bargemen – another of Ghent's guilds.

Map 1.2 - Walk to Number 10 which is two more doors down.

Korenlei 10 - The Swan

This was a brothel at one time and it has an impressive doorway. Look up to see the golden swans on the façade. They are facing away from each other - that tells us that the liaisons which took place there were for fun and business, not love.

Map 1.3 - Continue along Korenlei to reach number 15 on your right-hand side.

Korenlei 15

Number 15 is a beautiful white mansion on the site of what was once the courthouse.

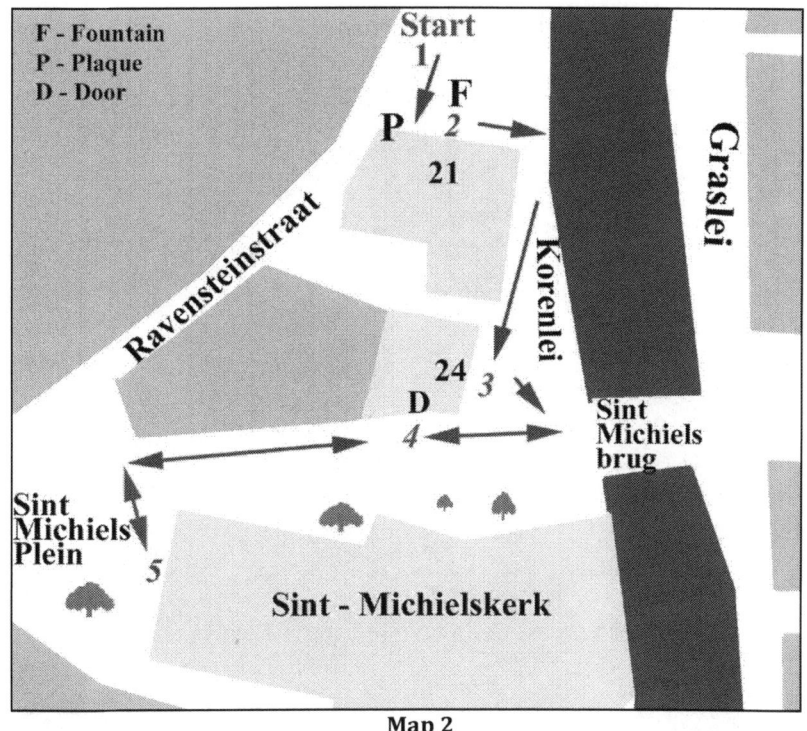

Map 2

Map 2.1 – A few more steps will bring you to another mansion at number 21. You will see a little fountain outside it.

Return of the Fountains

It is one of six old fountains around the city which were installed by the Society for the Protection of Animals in the nineteenth century.

They all have a bowl at the bottom for dogs, one in the middle for horses, and one for birds at the top. They have been recently been restored and put back into working order.

Number 21 - Portuguese Memorial

To the right of the mansion is a World War I war memorial, and on it are the coat-of-arms of Portugal and Flanders. It translates as:

> To the Portuguese soldiers
> who died on the Belgian front for the cause of law.

Every year on November 1st there is a ceremony in Ghent which names the nationalities of all soldiers who fought in World War I on Belgian soil.

Map 2.2 – Facing the front of the mansion at number 21, walk down its left-hand side and along the riverside towards Sint Michielsbrug.

The last building just before the bridge is number 24.

Number 24 – The Tapeworm

This building is much older than its neighbours. It has the year 1662 carved on the second floor, but that date refers only to the facade which was reconstructed in that year.

Map 2.3 - Climb the steps to reach the bridge. Turn right to walk away from the river and find a doorway at number 2 on your right.

Here you can see an older side of the same building. This huge fortress-like building was constructed from expensive limestone on an important and strategic position for a wealthy trading family.

It was called the Tapeworm which seems a very odd name to us, but in medieval times a tapeworm was a giant invincible snake-like dragon, and the name symbolized the strength of the fortress.

In the sixteenth century Philip II of Spain and his son Charles V visited Ghent. They and their entourage stayed in the Tapeworm.

Map 2.4 - The church on the opposite side of the road is St Michael's church. Walk downhill and away from the river to reach the front of the church. Hopefully it will be open, but it often isn't.

St Michaels church

This is Ghent's biggest church but it has had an eventful history.

We know that the first little chapel dedicated to St Michael existed way back at the start of the twelfth century. It burned down more than once but was always rebuilt.

It was replaced with a much bigger church in the fifteenth century, but as is often the case money ran out during its construction and work came to a halt. The church was then looted and badly damaged during all the religious upheavals of the sixteenth century.

When things quietened down it was reconstructed, and the plans included the addition of what was to be the highest tower in Flanders. But unfortunately money ran out again, so that part of the design was quietly set aside and forgotten about. We are left with just the stumpy base of the tower you see today.

Christ on the Cross – Anthony van Dyck

If you do manage to get inside, you will find "Christ on the cross" by Anthony van Dyck. You will have seen this scene many times by other artists. Mary is wearing her traditional blue cloak and Mary Magdalen is weeping at Jesus's feet. Mary Magdalen has her usual long blonde hair, regardless of how unlikely that was in real life.

The man on the right is holding up a stick which has a sponge soaked in vinegar as described in the bible. There is a lot of dispute over whether the sponge had a sedative in it to relieve the suffering, or whether it was just vinegar to add to the victim's suffering. No-one knows.

Map 2.5 - Leave the church and retrace your steps uphill to the river and to the bridge.

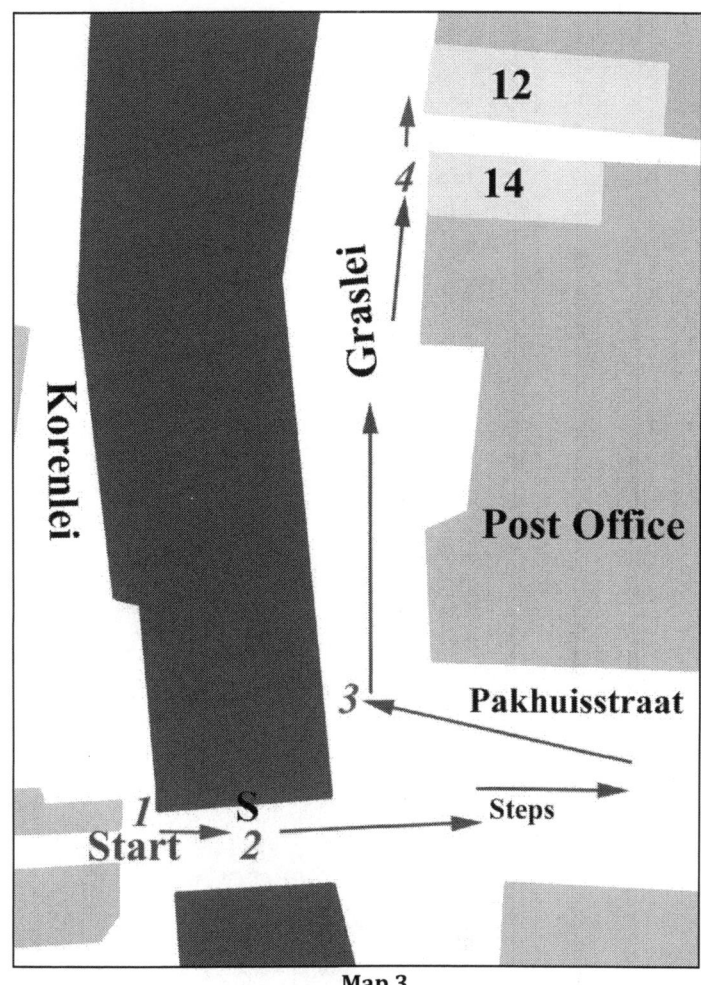

Map 3

Map 3.1 - Cross St Michael's bridge and enjoy the view of the towers of Ghent as you do. Pause about halfway over.

Saint Michael and the dragon

You will pass a very animated statue of the archangel Michael wielding a sword and slaying the dragon. It's on your left-hand side. It depicts a scene from the bible, the book of Revelations:

> And war broke out in heaven;
> Michael and his angels battled against the dragon.
> The dragon and its angels fought back,
> but they did not prevail
> and there was no longer any place for them in heaven.
> The huge dragon was thrown down to earth,
> that ancient serpent, who is called the Devil and Satan,
> the deceiver of the whole world -
> he was thrown down to earth,
> and its angels were thrown down with him.

Map 3.2 - Once over the bridge walk down the steps on your left-hand side. At the bottom of the steps turn left and you will reach the riverside once more.

Map 3.3 - Turn right to walk along Graslei - you can now get a closer look at the lovely buildings on this side of the river.

Walk past the rear of the post office to reach the buildings which were used to handle the cargoes being unloaded.

Stop at number 14 - it's the first building after the post office with steps leading up to the door.

Number 14 - The Guild House of the Free Boatmen

This is the guild house of the Free Boatmen. As mentioned already, their job was to transfer goods from the boats of the

Unfree Boatmen into their own boats and then bring them into Ghent – for a price of course.

The guild house has a lovely ship with masts, sails, and rigging above the doorway. The ship is a caravel, which is the same type of ship Columbus used to reach America. It also has lovely old stained windows on either side of the door, and the date 1531 just above the caravel.

The first floor is decorated with the coats of arms of the lands ruled by Charles V, and on the left-hand side is a sculpture of two swords emblazoned with his motto:

Plus Oultre
Always Further

On the second floor we see two sculptures of the Free Boatmen busy at work raising anchors.

Map 3.4 – A few more steps will bring you to number 12 next door.

Number 12 - First Grain measuring House

It advertises its function by having HET COOREMETERHUYS at the door.

This striking Gothic building was owned by the Grain Measurers guild and housed the scales which were used to weigh the grain arriving in Ghent. The guild controlled the amount of grain allowed to reach Ghent's market and they also set the prices the traders could charge.

You could take a look in the shop which is now installed in the Cooremeterhuys just to see the original old stonework and wooden beams.

Face away from the cooremeterhuys and look across the water to the canal-side brickwork opposite you.

Another Poem

You should be able to make out a line from the poem "Melopee" by Paul van Ostaijen inscribed on the brickwork.

Onder de maan schuift de lange rivier
Under the moon slides the long river

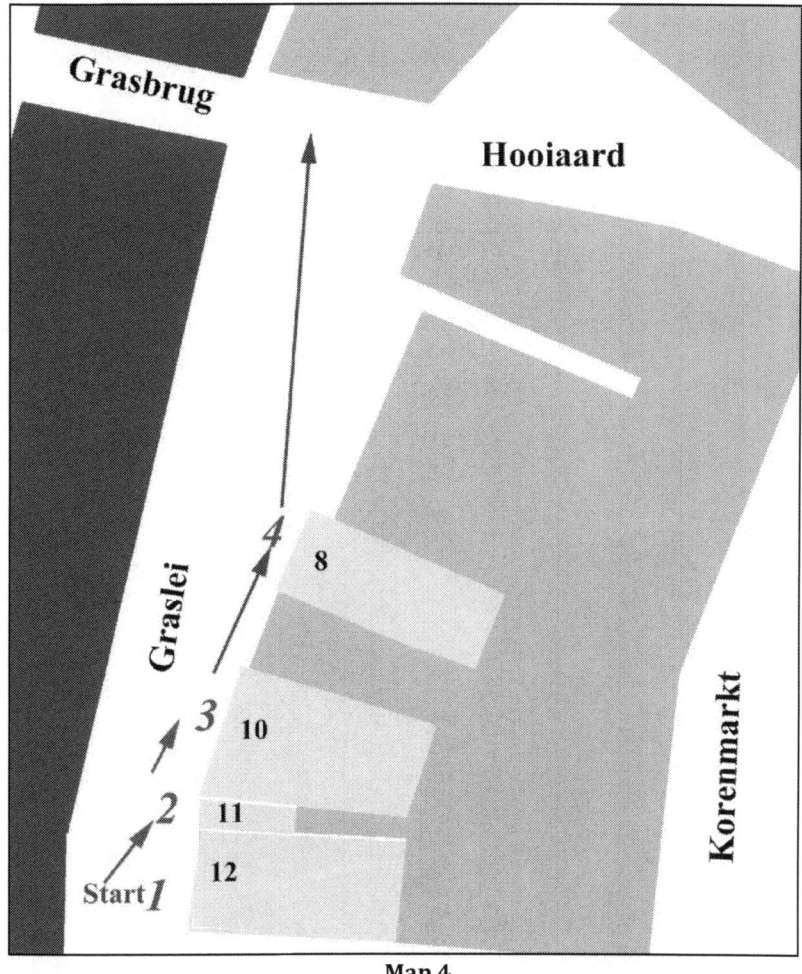

Map 4

Map 4.1 – Continue walking along to number 11 which is the tiny tollhouse next door.

Number 11 - Tollhouse

The city took a cut of all grain arriving in Ghent, and this is where the taxmen decided what their cut of the cargo would be.

Where the tollhouse stands used to be a little lane which separated the two much bigger buildings on either side. Some historians believe the lane was a firebreak in case of fire. Later the lane was used to house the tollhouse.

At the time of writing it is now a little café, so you could consider a visit. If you do, you will see what used to be the external walls of its two neighbours.

Map 4.2 - Just next door is the Spijker.

Number 10 - The Spijker

The huge dark grey building at Number 10 is the oldest house on Graslei, and it's thought to date from the twelfth century. It housed Ghent's grain store so that Ghent always had a buffer against famine. Notice the steps leading down to the entrance – that was street level when it was built.

The Spijker was completely restored at the start of the twentieth century. It's now a café so perhaps another dining possibility.

Map 4.3 - Now walk along to number 8. It's the next building with intricate carvings on its facade.

Number 8 - The Inghel

Number 8 gets its name from the angel bearing a banner on the facade.

Its facade is actually a copy of The Masons guild hall, which stands a few streets away and which you will see later. The Masons guild hall underwent a reconstruction in 1852, and it was generally thought that its original lovely facade had been lost. So when the Expo of 1913 was being planned, Ghent decided to replicate its original facade on this building on Graslei.

Later in 1976 they did some rework on the Masons guild hall itself, and they found that the original facade was still there – it was just buried under some plasterwork which has now been stripped. So we now have two buildings with the same facade. However the Mason's guild hall has something just a little bit special which you will see later.

Map 4.4 - Continue down the riverside until you reach the Grasbrug once more.

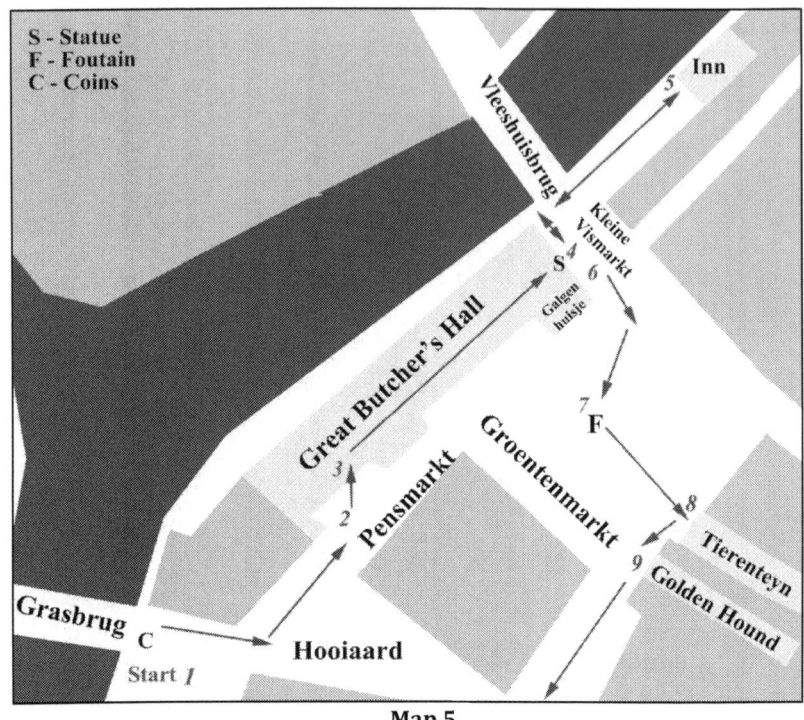

Map 5

Coin route

Look down at the cobbles at the start of the bridge on your left-hand side. You will spot a group of bronze "coins" which mark the start of the Coin Route.

It traces the route between the centre of Ghent and François Laurentplein which lies further east. It was part of the very important trade route between Bruges and Cologne in Germany.

The coins are each decorated with a historical image from Ghent's museums. This little group has some interesting images including a little map of Flemish cities and the Ghent coin route itself.

Map 5.1 - With the bridge on your left turn right into Hooiaard, but just a few steps and then turn left to walk into Pensmarkt.

It will take you along the back of the Great Butcher's Hall on your left hand side.

The Great Butcher's Hall

This building is clearly very old. It dates from the fifteenth century and it replaced an even earlier Butcher's Hall which was much smaller and built of wood.

Map 5.2 - Enter by the first open door you find to see the long hall with its wooden vaulted roof.

By law, meat could only be sold in Ghent in this hall, where the produce was monitored for freshness and quality. You can see a myriad of Ghent hams hanging from the rafters.

Map 5.3 - Walk right through the hall and emerge onto Kleine Vismark.

Turn round to see a colourful statue of Mary and Jesus above the Butcher's Hall door you just left by.

Mary and the Inkwell

Oddly Mary is holding an inkwell in her hand. It's time for another legend, and there are actually two tales to choose from.

Juul

The Night Watch discovered a body and by his clothes the victim had been a very wealthy citizen. The Watch was therefore very anxious to solve the case quickly, and by chance a meat carver named Juul was passing innocently by. The Night Watch questioned him and discovered that he had a large knife with blood on it. That was proof enough, and Juul was marched to the Gravensteen for interrogation.

Juul tried to explain that he had just slaughtered a pig but the interrogators preferred to believe that they had found the murderer. He was condemned to death next day.

Juul prayed all night until he fell asleep from exhaustion. He dreamt that Mary and the Baby Jesus appeared before him and that Mary had an inkpot in her hand. Jesus had a pen and paper and wrote something on the paper. He gave it to Juul with instructions to give it to the bailiff in the morning. Juul woke up and found a parchment beside him. He opened it and saw golden lettering – but he couldn't read so didn't know what it said. He asked to see the bailiff and handed over the parchment, the bailiff read it and ordered Juul's release immediately. No-one knows what the parchment said.

In gratitude Juul had the statue you see placed on the old Butchers Hall, and it was transferred to this Hall when it was built.

Huibrecht

Another popular story tells us about Huibrecht and his attempt to win a poetry competition. Huibrecht hit writer's block so his sister said a prayer for him. The Virgin Mary and baby Jesus appeared with an inkwell and a feather pen which they gave to Huibrecht. He was instantly inspired and wrote a masterpiece. Of course he won the competition and had this statue put up as a thank-you.

You can now take a little detour to an inn called The Waterhouse on the Beerside for refreshment.

Map 5.4 - With Mary behind you turn left to reach the bridge, but don't cross it. Instead turn right to walk along the riverside to reach this famous pub.

Waterhouse on the Beerside

It has over a hundred beers for sale – including Mammelokker, but it is also very much on the tourist trail, so you might want to just have a peep inside and decide if you fancy stopping for a beer, or perhaps returning another time

Map 5.5 - When you are ready to move on, retrace your steps along the riverside and turn left back into Kleine Vismarkt.

Pass Mary and her inkwell. Spot the little building stuck on the end of the Butcher's hall.

Galgenhuisje

It was there that the poor and desperate could buy tripe and entrails which were discarded from the Butcher's Hall.

It became the café Galgenhuisje in 1776 and is actually the smallest café in Ghent. Perhaps a chance for a refreshment in another unusual location.

Map 5.6 - Walk into the large square called Groentenmarkt which the café faces onto. In the middle of the square is an obelisk which holds a fountain.

Groentenmarkt

The water comes out of the mouths of the two faces on the sides. It was erected for the use of the fruit and vegetable sellers who sold their goods on this square. The fountain still works but its pump handle has been immobilized.

More Cuberdons

You might already have sampled cuberdons, but if not you get another chance now. There are two kiosks on this square selling this Ghent institution.

Urban Legend tells us that the stall owners are bitter rivals, and that they have tried various tactics in the past to outwit and out-market each other. So take your pick.

Map 5.7 - Stand with the Butcher's hall and the fountain directly behind you. Just ahead of you is a Ghent institution - Tierenteyn's mustard shop.

Number 3 - Tierenteyn

The Tierenteyn family has been making their own unique mustard since Napoleonic times. Since it was a labour intensive process to hand-grind the mustard, it was very expensive product and only the very wealthy could afford it. As the process became easier the price dropped and it became a favourite of everyone.

You might consider taking some home as a souvenir or a gift.

Map 5.8 - When you leave the shop, turn left to follow the tramlines into Kortemunt, but just a few steps. Pause at number 3 on your left – it's the second house along Kortemunt and has bow windows.

Kortemunt 3 - The Golden Hound

This building used to be called den Gouden Hund and it housed the most important tin foundry in Ghent which was owned by the De Keghel family.

It was in business until the start of the twentieth century and it produced handsome pieces of pewter which are still sold at auction houses today. When the foundry closed, the stock and the foundry equipment were bought by the House of Alijn Museum as part of Ghent's history.

If you have seen the Monuments Men movie, you will know about the theft of the Ghent Altarpiece and other precious works of art they could lay their hands on. The Germans were very efficient in appropriating anything of value, so they also stole the De Keghel moulds from the museum and they even took the tin which was still stored in the basement.

Map 5.9 – Continue in the same direction along Kortemunt to approach Korenmarkt.

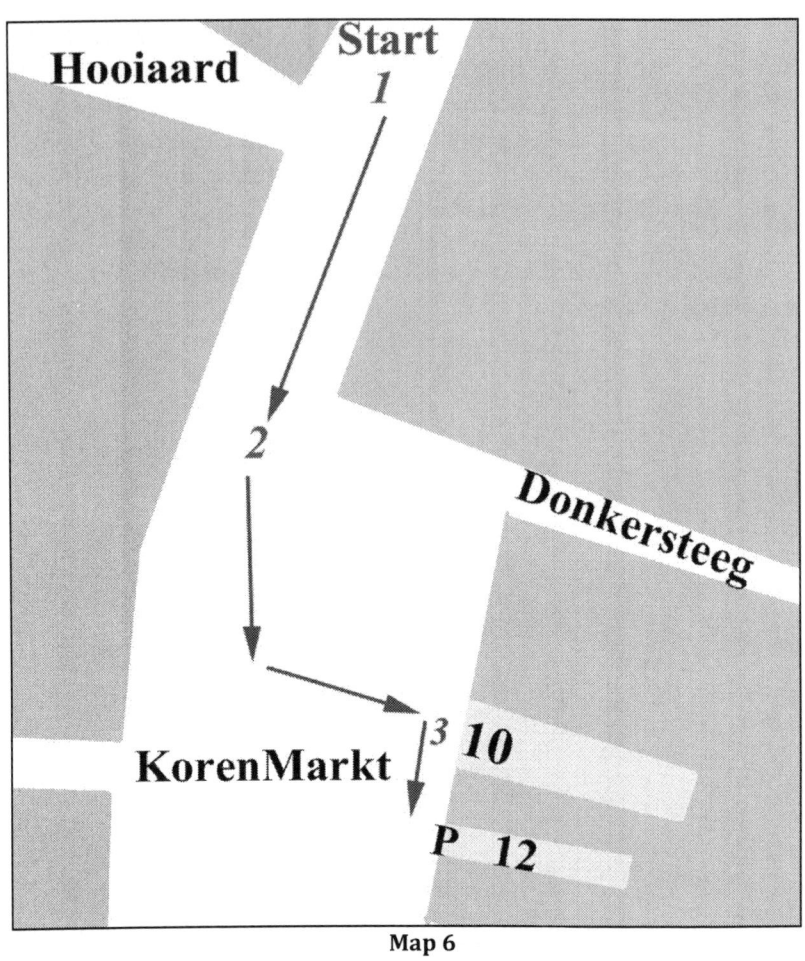

Map 6

Map 6.1 - You will see Little Ben ahead of you on your right, so walk towards it passing Hooiard on your right.

Map 6.2 - Enter the much wider KorenMarkt once more, passing Donkersteeg on your left.

Continue to follow the tramlines. Pause at number 10 on your left, it's the fifth building after Donkersteeg and it's the first one without a traditional stepped gable.

Société Anonyme des Timbres-Rabais

At the time of writing it is a restaurant but at the start of the twentieth century it was the Société Anonyme des Timbres-Rabais.

If you made a purchase at any affiliated shop you were given stamps, and if you saved them up and managed to accumulate enough you could come to this shop and exchange them for goods. The Society used to advertise in huge letters across the front of the building as:

> Everything free of charge
> Buy in the stores which give our stamps
> Our stamps are green – Beware of counterfeits

Map 6.3 – Walk along to number 12 which is just two buildings further along.

Quetelet

At the time of writing it's a burger bar.

Spot the plaque on the left-hand side of the door which has an image of Adolphe Quetelet.

He was born in this house and was a renowned mathematician and astronomer with many publications to this name. However he will better remembered as the man who devised the Quetelet Index, better known as the BMI, Body Mass Index, which tells us how fat people are. Belgium placed his image on a stamp in 1974.

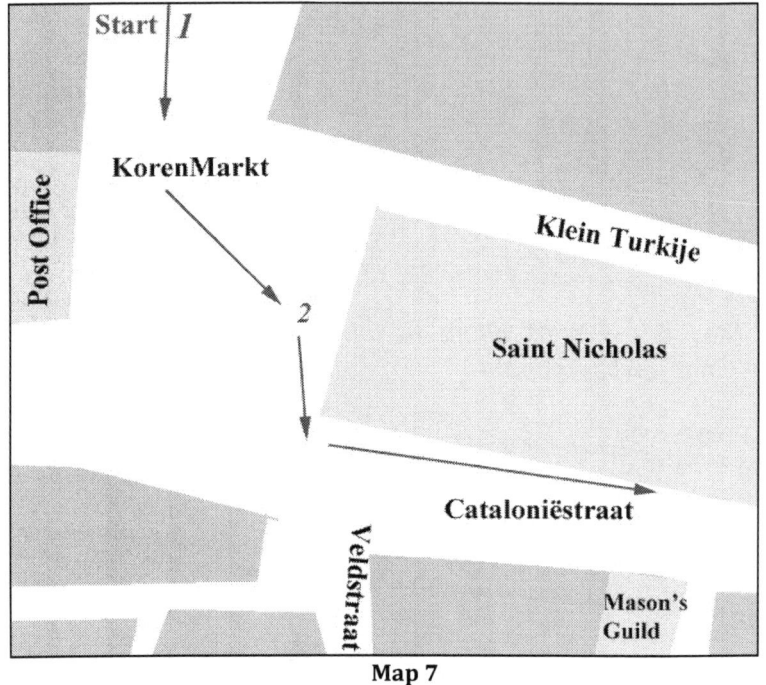

Map 7

Map 7.1 - Continue to the front of Saint Nicholas Church.

Map 7.2 - Face the front door of the church and go round the right-hand side into Cataloniëstraat. Walk to near the end of the church to find the original Masons Guild building on your right.

Mason's Guild Building

This is the building you read about earlier when exploring Graslei. It was thought to have been destroyed and since its façade was thought to have been so lovely, it was reconstructed on Graslei. It was later found that the original façade was buried under plasterwork and it has been restored.

You will see one major difference between how it was originally and now. It is now topped by six fascinating bronze devils that dance in the wind.

They are the addition of Ghent sculptor Walter De Buck and oddly they symbolise the worst aspects of humanity rather than the best.

You have now reached the end of this walk.

Did you enjoy these walks?

I do hope you found these walks both fun and interesting, and I would love feedback. If you have any comments, either good or bad, please review this book

You could also drop me a line on my amazon web page.

Other Strolling Around Books to try:

- Strolling Around Bilbao
- Strolling Around Arles
- Strolling Around Bruges
- Strolling Around Jerez
- Strolling Around Verona
- Strolling Around Palma
- Strolling Around Ljubljana
- Strolling Around Berlin
- Strolling Around The Hague
- Strolling Around Porto
- Strolling Around Lucca
- Strolling Around Amsterdam
- Strolling Around Madrid
- Strolling Around Lisbon
- Strolling Around Sienna
- Strolling Around Delft
- Strolling Around Florence
- Strolling Around Toledo
- Strolling Around Bath
- Strolling Around Antwerp
- Strolling Around Pisa

Printed in Great Britain
by Amazon